With clarity and compassion, Stu takes us on a journey into God's upside-down world. Don't read this unless you are ready to be wrecked for everything God loves.

GABE LYONS

Author of *Good Faith: Being a Christian When Society Thinks You're Irrelevant and Extreme* with David Kinnaman and founder of Q Ideas

When Jesus spoke the eight simple lines that we call the Beatitudes, he offered his listeners an alternate way to look at life, a different way to experience God. Stu Garrard invites us into a beautifully written, unfolding story to explore this unexpected way of living with God. He introduces us to people from the bright lights of the rich and famous to the shadows of death row who have each encountered this surprising transformation. I highly recommend *Words from the Hill* for those ready to join this journey.

TIM DAY

Author of *God Enters Stage Left*

Stu G writes like he plays. He weaves the new with the old, the passionate with the vulnerable. *Words from the Hill* is an honest, beautiful book from a man who paints with his fingers the stories that his heart perceives.

CRAIG BORLASE

Author of *Fleeing ISIS, Finding Jesus: The Real Story of God at Work* with Charles Morris, *10,000 Reasons: Stories of Faith, Hope, and Thankfulness Inspired by the Worship Anthem* with Matt Redman, and *Finding Gobi: A Little Dog with a Very Big Heart* with Dion Leonard

I can think of no one better to craft a story as in-depth as this one. Mark and I have known and loved Stu G and his family for many years. His approach to life has always been thought-provoking, creative, and generous, with a hunger for truth and a passion to continually communicate the pure gospel through the arts. Here

he explores the Beatitudes in all their depth and raw truth. I know this book and these songs will challenge and inspire you to find the unexpected blessings in the announcements of Jesus.

DARLENE ZSCHECH
Worship leader and singer-songwriter

Of all of Christ's teachings, few feel as timely and desperately needed today as the Beatitudes. Stu G has been courageously immersing himself in this deep stream for years. With keen insights, fresh language, heart-stretching stories, and the stunning melodies of an accompanying album, *Words from the Hill* is a unique and uniquely important invitation into the Way of Jesus.

AARON NIEQUIST
Worship leader and curator of The Practice and A New Liturgy

In *Words from the Hill: An Invitation to the Unexpected*, Stu Garrard captures the surprising and challenging call of the Beatitudes. Through inspiring artistry and compelling storytelling, Stu brings fresh eyes to this ancient text. What is particularly apparent is that Stu's own heart has been awakened to the beauty and confrontation of the words of Jesus. As highly involved members of our church, Stu and Karen continue to wrestle with what it means to live out these words right where they live. For years, Stu's friends have been telling him to write a book. Read this and find out why.

DARREN WHITEHEAD
Senior pastor of Church of the City and author of *Rumors of God* with Jon Tyson

stu garrard

WORDS
FROM THE HILL

an invitation to the unexpected

NAVPRESS

A NavPress resource published in alliance
with Tyndale House Publishers, Inc.

NavPress is the publishing ministry of The Navigators, an international Christian organization and leader in personal spiritual development. NavPress is committed to helping people grow spiritually and enjoy lives of meaning and hope through personal and group resources that are biblically rooted, culturally relevant, and highly practical.

For more information, visit www.NavPress.com.

Words from the Hill: An Invitation to the Unexpected

Copyright © 2017 by Stu Garrard. All rights reserved.

A NavPress resource published in alliance with Tyndale House Publishers, Inc.

NAVPRESS and the NAVPRESS logo are registered trademarks of NavPress, The Navigators, Colorado Springs, CO. *TYNDALE* is a registered trademark of Tyndale House Publishers, Inc. Absence of ® in connection with marks of NavPress or other parties does not indicate an absence of registration of those marks.

The Team:
Don Pape, Publisher
Caitlyn Carlson, Acquisitions Editor
Julie Chen, Designer

Cover illustration of hill by Julie Chen. Copyright © by Tyndale House Publishers, Inc. All rights reserved.

Hand lettering by Stu Garrard

Author photo by David Bean at visualreserve.com, copyright © 2016. All rights reserved.

For information about special discounts for bulk purchases, please contact Tyndale House Publishers at csresponse@tyndale.com or call 800-323-9400.

Cataloging-in-Publication Data is available.

ISBN 978-1-63146-598-7

Printed in the United States of America

23	22	21	20	19	18	17
7	6	5	4	3	2	1

To Karen,

for all the years of adventure, love, kindness, patience, and support.

CONTENTS

ACKNOWLEDGMENTS

I'VE BEEN DREAMING this book and project up for many years and am grateful for so many people:

My family: Karen, Kaitlyn (transcriber extraordinaire) and Adam, Cady and Vivi, Eden and Jordan. Our life together, the conversations and adventures we have, are like treasure to me.

Our parents: Thank you for believing in us, letting us fly and chase our dreams.

This book would not have been written without the belief, insistence, enthusiasm, and encouragement of Don Pape, my publisher; Caitlyn Carlson, my (very patient) editor; and the team at NavPress and Tyndale. Thanks are not enough.

Craig Borlase: Thanks for helping me find my voice at the beginning of this writing journey.

My friend and manager, Tony Patoto, who has helped make the dream of The Beatitudes Project a reality. Can't believe we still get to do this together. Thanks also to all the team at The Fuel Music Management Co.

My wise guides. These people are my compass points—blowing my mind, keeping me on track and true to the text since I'm a "feeler," not a scholar: Brad Nelson, Rabbi Joseph Edelheit, Tim Day, and Jim McNeish. Thank you all for the time, wisdom, and thought you have given to me, and also for letting me use your words.

Verdele Polson: for kindness and belief.

Todd Deatherage and the Telos Group: You have enabled me to meet people who embody these announcements in ways that I could not have imagined without you.

Jimmy Abegg: for hospitality, wisdom, music, art, and conversation around fire pits. You are an original collaborator!

The Jimmy A fire-pit crew—Steve Hindalong, Kevin Max, Cory Basil: Your friendship, art, and conversation have inspired this project more than you would know.

Darren Whitehead, pastor and friend: Thanks for helping us find family and a home at Church of the City, and for all the belief and support.

Scott Roley: for driving me around and showing me the side of Williamson County that is invisible to most people.

Daniel White: Thanks for connecting me with the amazing work of Food for the Hungry and for helping me to keep seeing God in the poor and the least. Also for late-night porch hangs.

Thanks to the spiritual guides who have been my lifeline and helped me navigate stormy waters: Al Andrews, Phil Portway, Jamie George, and Bill Hayley.

Henry and Alex Seeley: Thank you!

David and Donna Patterson and our TFH family: Thanks for everything—including the Stu G wing.

Michael W. Smith: Thank you, my brother!

Amy Grant: for saying yes, for lunch, for the song, the laughs, and the tears.

Jason Ingram and Paul Mabury: for friendship, music, incredible hospitality to a British immigrant, and belief in this book and project.

My former bandmates, Martin, Tim, Jon, Stew, and Paul: for all the years; the blood, sweat, and tears; the journey and the vision that shot us into this second half of life.

Troy Hatfield, Jacob Lowery, and Kevin Clay: for all the conversations into the early hours.

To all my many friends from the music world, worship communities, and movements that I've sat with over the last twenty years or so. All those conversations and questions and wisdom have helped form this journey and this project. It would be impossible to name check everyone, but please know that I am grateful and sincerely thankful to have been shaped by these moments with you.

Last and certainly not least, thank you to all the people who have let me tell their stories: Elissa, Sam, Tangie, Charles, Fady, Riyad, James, Jared, Darren, Becca, Regina, Jennifer, Dorris, Gaile, Roni, Daoud, Robi, Sami, Todd, Jeremy, Scott, Daniel, and Shane.

OF LIFE'S
UNEXPECTED PLACES

3:15 A.M. *Thursday, July 26, 2012. Emergency room, Vanderbilt Hospital, Nashville.*

I hadn't planned on this today.

It was supposed to be a quiet day. Maybe run a few errands, walk the dog, finish some edits I started yesterday. Maybe see if that new coffee shop is as good as people are saying it is. And yet here I am, sitting beside my wife in an emergency room.

Karen hasn't been well for a few weeks, so earlier today she finally went to the walk-in clinic. Nothing major, she thought, just the sort of unwell that would need a few pills to blast it away. The doctor thought otherwise. It only took a few minutes before he was telling her to go to the emergency room straightaway. He said she was the sort of unwell that needed some new blood.

We've been here for almost eleven hours. Karen's in a bed and I'm sitting beside her, trying to smile reassuringly. We're like an old couple. I thought we had decades ahead of us before we'd be comforting each other at a hospital bedside, but what can you do?

So far there have been tests and scans and consults with doctors who have perfect teeth and a warm, reassuring manner. They have told us that Karen needs surgery. We have told them that we have no health insurance.

Today has not gone how I expected.

Am I alone, or is this just how life goes?

We all experience those twists and turns. Some doors opening, some doors closing . . . it just happens. Life can change in an instant (or as we say in England, "turn on a sixpence!").

It just does.

Turns out Karen had a tumor the size of a tennis ball that was making her really sick. She was bleeding continuously. Thankfully the tumor was benign, and treatment straightaway, along with surgery to remove it in January 2013, was completely successful. But I know a lot of stories don't end that way.

That day in the hospital, I was thinking about Karen all the time. I wasn't complaining or feeling frustrated. The unexpected had completely interrupted my day, but that was okay. All that mattered was here and now and how to make Karen comfortable and get her better.

So I prayed. Not in an "I'm expecting a miracle" kind of way. Something more like "Help."

And in the midst of those terrifying hours, I had some kind of sense that God was not far away. There was something of the divine in the uncertainty, in the worry, in the hospital, in the here and now.

• • •

That day in the hospital happened in the middle of a lot of uncertainties, a lot of worries. In the middle of a huge transition.

It all started in 2008. I was in my forties and had spent the previous sixteen years in the job of a lifetime, making music with friends who were like family. And then, on a hot, muggy summer's day in Texas, we had a meeting that made clear that season was coming to an end. It was unexpected. It was hard. When the job ended in 2009, we were all trying to end well and treat one another as best we could, but I was already wrestling with God and a monster called Self-Doubt.

In 2010, I moved my family (complete with our dog, Buddy) from our home on the south coast of England to Nashville, Tennessee, and began making my way towards a new freelance career. A new country, a new opportunity . . . but very different ways of doing things in every single area of life. My visa said "Alien of Extraordinary Ability." I just felt like an alien.

Two years later, as Karen lay in that hospital bed, we weren't so different, she and I. I needed some new blood in my veins too . . . some fresh life.

Karen's new lifeblood came from refrigerated bags and incredible care from the staff at Vanderbilt. And mine? I started the journey to find mine when I began to accept that I am not in control. And there, at the bottom of all things, God met me.

Here's the thing. I want safety and comfort, but I have discovered that these are mere illusions sold to us by this modern life (and insurance companies). We all hope for the perfect outcome, but life doesn't follow our instructions.

This is nothing new. Jesus delivered what is considered to be his most complete sermon on this subject. We are not in control. Life does not always work out the way we expect it to. And, he tells us, when we find ourselves at the end of our rope, at rock bottom, God is there. God is on our side.

I began to find my new lifeblood in that sermon, and

particularly in the passage known as the Beatitudes, some of the most brilliant and poignant words ever spoken. In the midst of my uncertainty and this second act of my life, the one where nothing went as planned, these words took me over, consumed me, began to define how I looked at the world and how I responded to it. These words became an invitation to the unexpected. And they might just be the same for you.

•   •   •

But before we do anything else, I want us to consider a fascinating question my friend Rabbi Joseph asked me: *What does it mean to listen?*

I thought about that question, and I thought about the Beatitudes. What does it mean to listen like the people on the hill in the first century listened? There were no screens to read from, no devices to make notes on, no band to warm everyone up. Have we lost the ability to hear like that, to remember what we hear and put it into action in our lives?

I don't have the precise answer to this question of how to listen, but what I do have is my experience of being a musician onstage. And I think that perspective shows us something.

Onstage, we have a guide, which is the song. (In this instance, we have the Beatitudes.) Onstage, the musicians have to listen constantly to the rest of the band so they are always staying in harmony, not off playing music on their own. Listening—and learning—in community.

And in a band, it's not just a onetime performance. Just because the band plays successfully once doesn't mean they can rely on that for the future. They have to practice. They have to keep retuning their instruments. They have to keep playing the song.

So as we listen, as we learn how to listen, we need to replace certainty with humility, with curiosity. Because I can guess what some of you are thinking right about now: *The Beatitudes? I know all about the meek and poor in spirit and peacemaking stuff—it's good, sure, but I know all I need to know about it.* Right around the "Blessed are the . . ." we can tune out or nod our heads in acknowledgment and move on. But there's so much more. And we need to keep on discovering and pushing in, because this sacred text is living and breathing and full of permanent surplus meaning that will fill and make sense of life when it feels out of our control.

And how we get there might surprise us. Because it means listening in ways we don't usually listen when it comes to the Beatitudes. The invitation is to lift our eyes from the text for a moment, and from what we think we know of it. To lift our eyes from our devices, and see and hear these words in a different way.

See, I have some amazing people in my life, people who have encouraged and journeyed with me. People who have known me at my worst and at my best and have wanted to be my friend through it all, as well as new friends that I'm so lucky to have met. You will meet some of them in this book. And they'll help us see that the Beatitudes are not what so many people think they are. That these words are so much more than an instruction manual for living a good life, or some kind of spiritual ladder to climb.

As I've listened to our Teacher's words and to the people whose lives are living, breathing examples of them, I've realized something. Maybe there's a better way to read and live by these announcements. Maybe they could just offer us the most amazing good news you could ever hope to read: that God is always available to us and is fully present in the ache, the lack, the "not-yet-ness" of life.

I've sat on the hillside overlooking the Sea of Galilee where scholars tell us Jesus uttered these words, and in my mind I'm there now. Here is my invitation to you, from one broken human to another: If control is just an illusion, and life follows a different trail than the one we might have hoped for, how about we go exploring together? With Jesus' words as our compass and the insight from wise guides I've met along the way, how about we see if we can figure out some of the things that really matter in life?

Jesus has something for each of us here. It's time to release our need for control and accept his invitation to make sense of our days.

POOR IN SPIRIT

What You Find at the End of Your Rope

Loneliness and the feeling of being unwanted
is the most terrible poverty.

MOTHER TERESA

• • •

Blessed are the poor in spirit,
for theirs is the kingdom of heaven.

MATTHEW 5:3

• • •

You're blessed when you're at the end of your rope.
With less of you there is more of God and his rule.

MATTHEW 5:3, MSG

• • •

When darkness is our only friend
You are there
And we're longing for the hope of man
You will, you will, you will make a way.

"YOU WILL MAKE A WAY (POOR IN SPIRIT),"
ALL SONS AND DAUGHTERS AND STU G

MY MID-LIFE CRISIS began with the best of intentions. I wanted to make a difference, to take on some of the injustice in the world, to do something really *good* with my life. I just wanted to change the world for one or two people, that was all. That's how it all started. But it ended up nearly costing me everything.

I felt like I kind of used to be someone. I was part of a band that toured the world. We wrote songs for churches to sing, and we wrote songs for everyone else, too. Some even made it onto the charts. We had a passion and vision for big music that made a big sound for one big, united world, and we were going somewhere. Those were amazing years.

For the longest time our band was on an upward trajectory. We had a special "something"—some kind of prophetic imagination between us that doesn't happen very often. While not everything we did was a major success, our influence and audience were growing. The music business was still selling CDs in the '90s, so we were able to keep advancing and climbing by owning everything ourselves, employing a staff that felt like family, and building our own delivery systems. When we needed help, we partnered with others who were bigger and stronger. We liked those words, *bigger* and *stronger*.

For a time, we felt invincible.

I never really knew what poverty looked or felt like. Even though I came from a working-class background, my family was far from being poor. We had food on the table, a roof over our heads, and loving parents who stayed together and worked hard. Sometimes some of my friends had the fancy electric racing-car kit while I had the cheaper, gravity-controlled Matchbox set, but I didn't want for anything in terms of love and holidays and laughter. It was picture-postcard stuff, and it made me happy.

I left school as soon as I could. At sixteen years old I followed my dad into a manual trade, starting an apprenticeship with the Eastern Electricity Board. I thought I would be an electrician until the day I retired. I thought I had my career taken care of. Funny how these days, the very thought of having the same job, the same colleagues, and the same routine each and every day leaves me feeling nervous. But those were different days back then. Lots of people—myself included—were still hiding within the dream that the world was neat, predictable, and unchanging.

I got my wake-up call in September 1979 at Parrot Records in Ipswich. I was still sixteen, just a month into my apprentice-ship, feeling like a man with something to strut about. I was starting to like the feeling of having a little cash in my back pocket, and I'd walk around the streets of Ipswich wearing my mohair sweater and Doc Martens.

And then, in that record store, I heard Queen's album *Live Killers* for the first time. It changed my life. Literally.

I had been a Queen fan for years. Ever since I saw them per-form "Killer Queen" on *Top of the Pops*. There was just something about Freddie's voice and Brian's guitar orchestra that grabbed me in the gut.

But that day in Parrot Records, from the opening bars of "We Will Rock You," I knew that I wasn't just a fan. This was what I wanted to do. I didn't just like Brian May—I wanted to *be* Brian May.

So I went home, picked up my sister's nylon-strung classical guitar, and learned to play the Queen song "I'm in Love with My Car" by ear. I sold my drum kit that I had started to learn beats on, and I bought my first electric guitar. My black-walled bedroom became my rehearsal room and my concert arena all in one.

My fingers bled.

At twenty years old I married Karen, a bank clerk whom—I admit—I would whistle at as she walked past the building site I was working on as an electrician. Three years later we moved to London to pursue music. I was in a few bands, played a few sessions, and started working for my church as a musician and song leader. Karen and I had our first daughter, Kaitlyn, on a dark, rainy November night at Archway hospital in North London.

Somewhere along the way I met Tim Jupp and a young Martin Smith. I was drawn toward what they were doing on the south coast of England like a grain of space dust is drawn to a black hole. I found a home for my music there in Rustington, West Sussex, and together as a young family—we had our second daughter, Eden, on a bright spring day at Chichester hospital—we found a place to be and to grow.

Full of passion, vision, naiveté, and the Spirit, our band at The Cutting Edge events, and the cassette tapes we produced, paved the way for what became Delirious?

So we found ourselves travelling the world and sharing our music with millions of people in some really wonderful and interesting places.

And I remember Brazil.

We saw Jesus in Rio. Well, we *went* to see the statue, but I only saw his feet, as the rest of him was shrouded in mist. Then there was the Copacabana beach, samba dancing in São Paulo, sampling *picanha* in Brasília. We stayed in great hotels and saw everything the tourist office of Brazil wanted us to.

But then we saw the favelas—the slums that everybody

associates with Brazil. Filthy kids fighting for tiny scraps of food among the trash. Drugged and deformed beggars lining the streets. A dead man lying faceup in the middle of the road, his eyes staring heavenwards.

I didn't feel safe there. But the danger wasn't external—it was internal. This five-star musician lifestyle just didn't seem to fit with what I was seeing, let alone what I was singing.

I felt challenged and extremely uncomfortable. The sort of uncomfortable you feel when you're in a skid and about to crash into a tree—you're not in control and you know what's about to happen. Up until now, being a Christian had been about waiting for God to show up at the gig and not getting in the way as the "power flowed." But now to watch from the stage wasn't enough. I was learning the story that's always been true: the story of the God who hears the cries of the oppressed, those enslaved by lack of power and choices, and I felt the pull toward the unexpected—a new way of being. To join that story and *do something*.

So I went home and put an offer in on a better, bigger house, closer to the beach, with more rooms and a space for a studio in the garden.

• • •

I hated India when I landed there for the first time. I don't say that lightly—I really did hate it. Every sense was on edge, overwhelmed by the smell of sweat and cheap petrol engines, the sound of traffic and too many people shouting, the heat, the taste of poverty, the sight of so much chaos. So many people crowding, jostling, wanting to carry our bags even before we had gotten near the airport doors. Then outside, the beggars, the street people all wanting something from the rich Westerners walking out with guitars in expensive-looking flight cases.

The air-conditioned car ride to the air-conditioned hotel was like being decompressed after a deep-sea dive. But it didn't make me feel any better. There were armed guards outside the hotel, but they didn't make me feel any safer. Were they meant to stop the outside world from getting in, or were they there to stop me from getting out?

Finally, alone in my hotel room, I stared at the mirror.

What are you doing here? I asked myself.

I called Karen. I felt like a kid suddenly pole-axed by home-sickness while on a school trip. "I just wanna come home," I told her.

"Stu, just go and be you," she said. "Be kind to people, do your job, and then come home."

There's nobody like Karen for putting my head back on straight.

Next morning a few friends and I jumped in *tuk tuks* and explored the city of Hyderabad. What did I have to lose? It seemed somehow different in the sunlight. We walked out of our five-star dream and immediately noticed a pristinely and colorfully dressed woman outside the blue tarpaulin shack that was her home, sweeping the road with a few twigs.

We dodged in and out of the ridiculous traffic, accompanied by the auto-horn symphony, breathing in the two-stroke *tuk tuk* fumes. Watching the crazy theater of Hyderabad kick off in front of our eyes and ears was intense. A new sound, a bold image . . . every few seconds something else pulled my head towards it.

I was holding on for dear life. But what kind of life?

Later on that trip we played a concert in Mumbai and visited a feeding program for kids of sex workers in the vast slums there. Millions live beneath the blue tarpaulin and rusty tin homes, straddling open sewers, fighting for life against all odds. Those broken, beautiful people embedded themselves in my heart. Prostitutes and their kids, transvestites, and the folks giving their lives to serve these people in dire poverty—they all fused together within my mind, a crazed symphony of suffering and hope. So many of my fears, my prejudices, my stupidly simple answers, my Western privilege, and my easy, simple religion died there that day.

And I fell in love with India. I fell in love with it the way I fell in love with my wife when I saw her though the glass door, before she could see me, on our second date. I fell in love the way parents fall in love with the hazy, black-and-white image on the shiny bit of paper that the sonographer hands them in the darkened room. All that risk and all that hope. All that potential and all that chaos.

It sounds strange to me now, but I think I fell in love with India most of all because it was there that I finally saw God, in the very people I had never really noticed before. When I finally stopped and stared at the poor and the least, the weakest and the last, I saw his love and compassion in action.

And it was I who felt poor.

What was I supposed to do with all this? I was coming apart at the seams.

And when it became clear a few months later that the band was going to end, I may have been coping on the outside—but on the inside, I went into free fall.

• • •

If you want to see where God is, look at the Beatitudes.

Let's put ourselves on the hill that day. Jesus was looking at the very people he was talking about. And if you were going to go look for the "blessed" of the world, you wouldn't go looking there!

But embedded in these amazing words is the key to finding where God is closest to us: in the places we're least likely to look.

The other day, I came across this hard reality: Nearly half the world's population—2.7 billion people—live on less than $2.50 a day. And 1.2 billion live in extreme poverty—less than $1.25 a day.[1]

It's hard to believe, isn't it?

The vast and growing gap between rich and poor has been laid bare in a new Oxfam report showing that the sixty-two richest billionaires in the world own as much wealth as the poorer half of the world's population.[2]

When I read this, I feel sick to my stomach.

I spend more on a single cup of coffee than 1.2 billion people alive right now have to live on per day.

It's easy to imagine that more than half the people on the planet are not only poor but living with crushed spirits.

Trite language such as "You have the power to change your life" is so inappropriate for most of the planet. The gap between the mega-rich and the extremely poor is sickening and wrong.

It's almost like it's been designed to keep people in their place.

And yet how can I even comment on this, a guy who wishes he were a millionaire every day?

But I wrestle.

The thing is, once you've "seen," you just can't "un-see." It never leaves you, nor should it. It disrupts you for life.

Since the slums of India, the favelas of Brazil, the waste dumps of Cambodia . . . life has not been the same. A daily wrestle with very few answers.

And then there are those of us with money in the bank, stuff in our houses—and the suffocating darkness and depression of feeling empty and unsatisfied. A different poverty of spirit, but spirit crushing nevertheless. Matthew's Jesus makes sure these people are also included.

Let's make no mistake. Jesus announces first and foremost that if you are poor—whether materially or deep in your soul—and it has crushed your spirit, God is on your side. No requirements, nothing to attain. This is the situation right now. Whoever you are. Wherever you are.

We don't have to look very far. I've been privileged to travel, and I have seen the most amazing people in the direst circumstances, and observing their resilience and joy has changed me forever. But I can also walk a couple of miles from my house in one of the most desirable counties in America and find neighborhoods where if the schools didn't send the kids home with food for the weekend, they would go hungry.

Unbelievable.

Hard to see a blessing.

And it's nothing to be earned.

It's just what *is*.

God is on their side.

ELISSA KIM

I met Elissa Kim through something called Q Commons, which is a local expression of Q Ideas, an organization formed by my friend Gabe Lyons. Q helps folks engage in conversations that are all too easy to shy away from.

At Q Commons, Elissa was talking about her work with Teach For America, and her story and her passion for her job and the low-income communities she works with really inspired me. I was able to get in touch with her and meet up over a coffee in East Nashville to go deeper into her story.

Elissa is one of four children born to South Korean immigrants living in Indiana. Both her parents came from incredibly poor families.

Rising from the ashes of World War II, her mother's father had made the journey down south to scrape around for work. But then the Korean War broke out, and the north/south border was created. He met and married his wife in the south but never saw any of his family in the north again.

None of Elissa's grandparents could read or write, but her father's parents decided that they would sacrifice everything they could to give him a basic education. So they worked and worked and sacrificed and pushed doors so their son could learn to read and write.

Well, he turned out to be quite the bright kid. After some exam success, he got himself into med school, and from there he joined the army as a medic.

Elissa says that without the sacrifice of her grandparents and the "miracle" of basic education, her father would have lacked choices and therefore opportunities. His parents could see that education was the "key" needed to open doors to the choices they never had. He clearly had talent, but in the absence of the most basic education it wouldn't have mattered.

Elissa's parents had an arranged marriage, and it wasn't too long before they emigrated to the States, where Elissa's dad became a doctor. Then a couple of things happened that changed the Kim family's course again. Elissa's dad was in a serious car crash that all the cops and medics said he shouldn't have survived, much less walked away from. He was so shaken up, he said, "I was saved for something."

Later, he contracted lupus so serious that it put him on his deathbed. With friends gathered around and Elissa's mum crying, the physicians came into the room and said there was nothing left they could do. They were trying to prepare Elissa's mum to be a single mother taking care of four kids. How would they survive?

But weeks later, Elissa's dad pulled through—and thought for a second time, *I'm intended for something.*

"So he started exploring what he should do," Elissa says, "and he felt led to Kazakhstan first. And then he ended up opening free medical clinics in Uzbekistan, providing free medical care to the poor—and he did that for twenty years."

So this guy who brings his family out of poverty—through the chance of a basic education—becomes a doctor, and then gives free medical care to the poorest of the poor using his own money, in another country, for twenty years. Unbelievable!

But that's not the end of the story.

Elissa grew up in this household in Indiana that placed a high value on education, and there was never a question about whether the kids would go to college. Elissa got a full-ride athletic scholarship to play tennis at Northwestern University in Illinois.

Her own story differed from her father's in that she didn't really lack privilege growing up—but once she made it to the university environment, she quickly realized how much the circumstances of birth dictate the opportunities that people get.

The university culture is highly pre-professional, and so it's a bunch of hypereducated, privileged kids who really do have the world in front of them. They know they are going to get a great education, they can choose to go to Wall Street, they can choose to go to law school, they can choose to start their own business. They can do whatever they want, and these were the things that the system valued. Elissa fell in that path and said, "Okay, I'm supposed to be a lawyer."

To her it was at least a recognized path, and maybe she'd figure out what she was supposed to do with her life later on. Elissa says,

> In my junior year, a sorority sister of mine who was graduating got accepted into this program called Teach For America. I had never heard of it before. She was so excited about it—committing to teach for two years, working hard and making sure that kids in low-income communities get the kind of education they deserve. From the second that description rolled out of her mouth I was hooked. When senior year rolled around, I applied, got in, and said, "Okay, I'm gonna do this for two years and *then* go to law school."

Then of course what happened—which happens to just about everyone that joins Teach For America—is that I walked in thinking I was gonna take one path . . . and then I met my kids, fell in love, became completely outraged by what I saw. I mean, I taught in the largest public high school in New Orleans, and I had kids who couldn't read. I couldn't believe it. These brilliant, brilliant kids, very talented. They clearly had the intellectual and cognitive chops to be able to do it, and the system had completely failed them. When you see that, your life changes. All I could see was my dad. Same level of talent. The only thing is that my dad got a couple lucky breaks and a couple of opportunities. So that set me on a totally different path.

I ended up teaching for three years, then getting recruited to New York to join the organization. I thought, *Well, maybe I could have an influence on the system.* For the last seventeen years, I've been leading the recruitment effort for Teach For America. My job is to find people like me to join and to do what I did, and over the last seventeen years, 50,000 people have joined TFA. The vast majority of those people have come in under my watch.[3]

So, time-out for a second. A man brings his family out of extreme poverty in one generation through the sacrifice of his parents and the "miracle" of a basic education, and he goes on to give himself back to the poorest of the poor. Then his daughter is so impacted by the lack of opportunity for the poor within the education system that she leaves the career ladder to help provide the kind of educational opportunities her dad got.

How extremely cool is that?

Sounds great, you may be thinking. *But I can't quit my job and join Teach For America. I have to provide for myself, for my own family. Poverty is sad, but I'm not in a place to do anything about it.*

And sure, no one person or one way has the solution to the poverty in the world. But we all have a part to play. Society tells us, "If you're smart and intelligent, you should only do this handful of things." And we just go with the flow, doing what's expected, feeling empty, lacking purpose. But recognizing our own poverty is the start of learning how to play our part.

During her time in New Orleans, Elissa had a student whose family was so poor that the only shirt he had was his school shirt. But when she visited this kid and his family—and all these kids and their families—or went to church with them or went out with them on the streets at Mardi Gras, she was struck by the joy they had in community and in one another. Elissa said, "It made me feel like maybe it was me that was impoverished. One can be rich in many different ways, and one can be poor in many different ways."[4]

My friend and manager Tony Patoto and I were mulling over Jesus' language of "poor in spirit" and how, though he is probably talking about the actual poor, his choice of words widens the arc. Life doesn't always turn out like we expect it to. Sometimes we can have all our physical and material needs met, and yet we still experience a crushing of spirit, a lack or an absence—a different form of spiritual poverty.

SAM POLK

In my last year on Wall Street my bonus was $3.6 million— and I was angry because it wasn't big enough. . . . I wanted

more money for exactly the same reason an alcoholic needs
another drink: I was addicted.[5]

I stumbled across these words in the *New York Times* the other
day—and Sam Polk had my attention! Through the wonders of
the Internet I managed to get in touch with Sam, and I got to
hear his whole story.

When Sam was growing up, his dad instilled in him the
belief that money would solve all his problems. "Imagine what
life will be like when I make a million dollars," his dad would
say.[6] And so when Sam walked onto the Wall Street trading floor
for the first time, he knew what he wanted to do. The hectic
rush of the floor promised the one thing he'd always wanted:
to be *rich*.

Sam had come through Columbia University competitive
and ambitious, but he was also regularly drinking, smoking
pot, and using cocaine, Ritalin, and ecstasy. He got a presti-
gious internship—but he lied to do so. He didn't want to miss
out on this chance for a step up the ladder. His then-girlfriend
dumped him three weeks into the internship. "I don't like who
you've become," she said. Sam couldn't blame her. He sought
out help for his alcohol and drug use, and his counselor told
him that his "abuse of drugs and alcohol was a symptom of . . .
a 'spiritual malady.'"[7]

After his final year at Columbia, he got a job with Bank of
America. With a year of sobriety under his belt, he was sharp,
clear-eyed, and hardworking. At the end of that first year,
he received a bonus of tens of thousands of dollars. Sam was
thrilled—but jealous of a friend who was hired away by Credit
Suisse First Boston for almost a million.

And so Sam worked even harder, climbing the Wall Street ladder. He became a bond and credit default swap trader, and just four years later, Citibank offered him a job worth millions.

But he was still nagged by envy: "When the guy next to you makes $10 million, $1 million or $2 million doesn't look so sweet."[8]

And then he began to notice something. The folks he worked with on Wall Street were afraid of losing their money, and they would do anything to protect their bonuses, despising anything or anyone that would get in their way. It was like watching a drug addict desperate for the next fix. "For the first time," Sam wrote in the *New York Times*, "I was embarrassed for them, and for me. I made in a single year more than my mom made her whole life. . . . Not only was I not helping to fix any problems in the world, but I was profiting from them."[9]

Sam decided to leave Wall Street, but it was incredibly hard. He was petrified of losing his money. And then his bosses said they'd raise his bonus, but only if he stayed several more years.

But Sam walked away.

"I think I was a good person," Sam says. "I was clearly doing something that wasn't contributing to the world in a really good way, but when I hear folks talk about people on Wall Street, they think they're all criminals. They're not all criminals. They're just normal, working people—but I do think that they and I were basically standing in the wrong place. The circle of compassion was very small."[10]

In the time since he left, Sam's gotten married, spoken in jails and juvenile detention centres about getting sober, taught a writing class for girls in the foster system, and started a non-profit called Groceryships, which is a brilliant work helping the poorest of families put healthy food on the table. And he's also partnered in a new start-up business venture called Everytable, which is dedicated to making nutritious meals available in "food deserts"—communities who lack access to healthy foods and experience high rates of obesity, diabetes, and stress—at afford-able prices.

This is what really compelled me to want to tell Sam's story in the first place. The obvious change of direction, realizing his own poverty of spirit, transforming his story into one that is helping others.

I asked Sam what "poor in spirit" means to him, and he told me about a recent conversation he had with a friend who had left his own hedge fund job. The man told Sam, "I realized a lot of money just makes you comfortably miserable."

Sam thinks that is exactly what poverty of spirit looks like to the mega-rich. He believes that there's a sickness on Wall Street. Not that these people are evil, but that they're living with an emptiness, a missing connection to something that's greater than themselves, whether it's God or humanity or a purpose.

And *in* that emptiness, *in* that lack of connection . . . God announces that he is on our side.

THE GIFT

My appointment was for 10:00, but I was there at 9:45. I always like to be early. The therapist worked from an office out the back of a charity store, so I was able to pretend to check things out for a while before the session started. I disguised myself behind shelves of ethically sourced coffee and waited. When 10:00 came around, the door at the back of the shop opened and I watched as it released two people: The woman looked a little like my sister, while the man was a short, stout Londoner. The woman left, and the man joked around with the other woman working on the cash register. He seemed different from a lot of people I knew at the time. He seemed happy.

So this was Phil, my therapist. We'd not met before. I'd met other therapists in my life, but never for professional reasons. Maybe that's why I was feeling nervous. I checked my bag again. It was always with me, and I knew exactly what was in it: a notebook, a novel, gum, hand sanitizer, lip balm, a phone, cigarettes. (I'd taken to smoking but didn't realize it was because it helped me stop and breathe deeply for a moment. I could have done that without tobacco, but there you are.) Checking my bag made me feel better.

It occurred to me that I might look like a potential thief, hiding out behind the shelves while at the same time searching through my bag, so I decided to check out some of the other products that the shop sold. I was genuinely taken with a nice little French press when I noticed someone was standing next to me.

"'Ello, mate," said Phil. "Fancy a coffee, then?"

I mumbled something and followed him back to his room.

No windows to the outside world. Three chairs. Tissues in a box on a low table to the side.

I opened my bag as he made the coffee. I had some notes already made—mainly about what I thought my problems were and how it would be good if Phil could just help me fix them up. He smiled as I talked him through it all.

"I just want to make everything better," I said.

"Everything?"

"Y-es," I said, slowly, trying to work out whether it was a trick question.

"Okay. Let's talk about your bag, Stu."

It turned out that Phil wasn't talking about my actual bag. He was talking about my baggage. In the minutes—and the weeks—that followed, he showed me that while I thought I had a neat little list of issues I needed to work through, what I really had was a bag full of spiritual and emotional troubles that I had been carrying around with me for far too long. They were heavy, and I was tired from all that lifting. Slowly—very slowly—Phil showed me how to lessen the burden.

See, most people have two identities. There's the false self, whom you put on show and update your Twitter and Facebook accounts with, and then there's the true self—the one who stays mostly hidden in the shadows, hiding back there with your secrets and stories that you really don't want to put on show. Keeping the false self apart from the true self takes a lot of effort, and when one of them starts to crumble, the other one struggles as well.

I had two selves. I was Stu G the guitarist, songwriter, and professional Christian. And then I was Stuart Garrard, the ginger kid from Suffolk. Trouble was, even though he was a professional Christian, Stu G was the false self. And he was falling apart.

I had been aching for so long. Being Stu G meant wearing an "I'm okay" mask for so much of the time. It meant feeling desperate and feeling scared, and it left me clinging to some relationships in ways that were not at all helpful for anyone involved. It meant life was all messed up, and my neat little list of issues that I'd scribbled on a single page of my note-book didn't come anywhere near describing the damage.

That first session ended with me taking what felt like the deepest breath I'd ever taken—the sort that threatens to burst your lungs wide open. But they didn't burst. They held firm. And then came the exhale. All that stale air, the stuff that no longer gave me life, blown out from my body, making room for new life, for fresh air.

"Failure's a gift," said Phil as the final minute counted down. "When you can't fix it, you don't need to fix it."

I left, walking past the coffee and the nice-looking French press, got outside, and breathed again.

• • •

I've met so many people like me. So many of us whose lives are tangled up, so many who are recovering but still limp-ing. So many of us who aren't among the world's poorest, like Elissa's family, or the world's richest, like Sam—and yet we feel as though we're scraping out an existence just to stay alive. So many of us who are carrying so much spiritual and emotional baggage that our bones are bent with the weight. So many of us who have forgotten what it feels like to breathe freely or to just be ourselves. Or to be happy.

And while our symptoms and our causes are as unique as the freckles on our skin, we're all united by one simple word: *poverty*. We're all poor. None of us can make it on our own.

And it is precisely at this point—the one where we begin to feel the rope slipping too fast from our hands, its coarse fibers burning our soft flesh—that we are handed the gift of failure. And there we find God.

As I walked back past the shelves of ethical coffee week after week, gradually it dawned on me that the God I was struggling to follow was not angry or disappointed or distant. Somehow, I had this living, vibrating, visceral sense that God was with me—despite (or was it because of?) the fact that I was poor in spirit.

God is on the side of everybody for whom there's no reason why God should be on their side. Sometimes we have to ask the seemingly unanswerable questions before we can be ready for the answers. And right there in the middle of the world's most famous sermon ever is the key to making sense of life.

Not just first-century Palestine life either. This twenty-first-century life, with all its collisions and chaos, all its hypocrisy and hope, all its poverty and potential.

You are blessed when you are

- poor,
- poor in spirit,
- spiritually bankrupt,
- pathetic,
- bedraggled,
- confused,
- morally empty,
- believing the lie that there's nothing good left within you.

Because the God who is reordering, remaking, restoring, and reshaping the world is with you.

God is on your side.

MOURN

The Grief of Change

The flight from sorrow leads to
the loss of hope.

AL ANDREWS

•   •   •

Blessed are those who mourn,
for they will be comforted.

MATTHEW 5:4

•   •   •

You're blessed when you feel you've lost
what is most dear to you. Only then can you
be embraced by the One most dear to you.

MATTHEW 5:4, MSG

•   •   •

Rolling waves of sorrow
Rivers of grief
In the valley of the shadow
I feel you walking with me.

"CARRY ON (MOURN),"
MICHAEL W SMITH, IAN CRON, AND STU G

I WANT TO TELL you about Joe.

Joe Cox was my best friend. I was his apprentice for most of my four years of training as an electrician. For some reason, I excelled at my college studies as part of my apprenticeship, and when the Eastern Electricity Board wanted me to become an engineer (which I now realize was a huge career move), I declined because I didn't want to leave working in a team with Joe. I guess I've always wanted to be in the band!

For four years or so we worked together most days. He taught me all he knew, even how to fish for cod off the beaches of the cold, grey, windy east coast of England. We froze our butts off but sang and danced to Rod Stewart on the pebbles in the cold grey mist.

When Joe was in hospital for surgery to remove a piece of chipped bone in his knee, I visited him every day.

When I got married, Joe was my best man—I laughed at seeing him in a suit, having to be all "proper."

He was there for me like no one else (other than my dad), always available on the other end of the phone to give advice, electrical or otherwise.

When I left the Eastern Electricity Board and our hometown in the East to move to London and chase my musical dreams, we talked every week.

So when a former colleague called me to say that Joe had been killed in a motorcycle accident, time stood still.

It was beyond anything I had felt or experienced before.

An exhausting, lonely ache.

At Joe's funeral I numbly talked with his family and my former workmates. It was all too much at the graveside. As Karen and I stood there, Josey, Joe's wife, fell into our arms, crying, "I didn't want Joe to die."

We wept.

Karen and I were part of a church community in London that believed in miracles. The fact that God felt "real" there, in the way that people loved each other and lived in connectedness, was what attracted us to becoming Christians as young twenty-year-olds. We had a communal lifestyle—several families living together, all of us sharing purse and sharing life. And we had a simple belief that God could do anything.

So when the sad crowd left the graveside to head to Joe and Josey's house, I ran back to the graveside to be on my own for a moment with Joe. I was devastated to see that six feet of soil had already been dumped back on top of my best friend.

But God can do anything, right?

With the rain leaking through the layers of my suit and the dark grey clouds rolling across the sky and through my soul, I prayed like I had never prayed before, with groans and tears . . .

And I tried to raise Joe from the dead.

Nothing happened.

• • •

The other day I watched the U2 show from Paris. The one rescheduled after the terror attacks that killed 130 people in November 2015.

I love U2. Always have. My favorite album is *Zooropa*. I don't meet many folks who would agree, but I identify with the wrestle in that record. I love how U2 have grown and moved and flexed with the years. I love how they have a voice and do their best to use it for those who don't get to have a microphone. I love the poetry in the lyrics, and for me as a guitar player, The Edge has been an inspiration with his sonic architecture. I'd love to meet them one day.

But as I watched that Paris concert with all its poignancy and messages of support for Paris, urging Europe to stay with heart and arms wide open to the refugees and migrants flooding in from around the world, what began as a feeling of euphoria turned into an ache of sadness.

I stopped myself for a moment because it felt like envy.

How come they can still be doing this after forty years when Delirious? didn't quite make it to twenty?

It made me miss Delirious? Not that we were as big as U2, but it was seventeen years! And in that moment, watching TV, I missed the raw passion, the vision, the sense that we were going somewhere and saying something. I missed playing the music we'd written together, and I missed standing alongside Martin at the front of the stage, helping to steer a movement with prophetic vision. I just missed it. It's gone.

It's a loss that maybe I hadn't fully faced or grieved, although I thought I had . . . maybe this was just an aftershock. It was an ending that changed my course, and looking back I thought I was coping as best I could—but I tried to get past it as quickly as possible, perhaps at the cost of truly going through it.

I tried to numb the feelings, distract them with other things. Good things, like finding out what was next and embarking on a new career, knowing that there has to be more where that came from. Not-so-good things, like trying to cling to relationships and connections like driftwood to avoid drowning. I should have let go and trusted that I would fall into an ocean of love, but all I could see was a sea of sorrow. So I tried to take control and manipulate it all, and I just made it worse. Until I ended up in Manger Square in Bethlehem . . . but that story's coming later.

And in all those feelings—sadness, envy, regret for the mistakes I made—even while the ache was strong . . .

I didn't feel alone.

THE GOD STORY

I tell those two stories not because they are the perfect explanations or best examples of this mourning beatitude, but simply because they are mine.

You will have your own personal and painful stories of grief, of the change that it brought, of the wounds you carry and the healing that is ever ongoing.

At the end of the day, grief is different for everyone. And what makes pain so unbearable is the way that it isolates us from one another. We try to bring a crumb of comfort by saying things like "I know how you feel," but even if we have been through a similar experience, those words are trite and untrue. How can we possibly know how someone else feels? We can *relate*, but we can't *know*, because it's so different for everyone. So maybe the best alternative we have is to join people in their sadness and their loss and their rage.

And this really is the God story. The story of the one who hears the cry of the victim, the hurting, the broken. God hears the blood of Abel crying out from the ground. He goes to Sodom and Gomorrah to investigate the "outcry" that reached him. He hears the groans of the Israelites in misery and slavery. Throughout the story of Scripture, God hears the cry and draws near. It's like he can't help himself—he cannot resist the cry of the brokenhearted, the victim, and the vulnerable. He is drawn to their side.

Whenever I read, "Blessed are those who mourn, for they will be comforted," I automatically think about the loss or death of someone close, someone we can't bear to be apart from. This pain and ache feels way too deep down in the soul to ever recover from. The grief that comes with that kind of loss, especially if it feels too soon, is beyond words. But grief is also more than that.

David Kessler says that the way we experience grief is as unique as our fingerprint.[1] He has spent years helping people— from those who are dying and their loved ones, to those who are coping with divorces and breakups, to victims of plane crashes and multiple shootings. He says that whatever our grief is, it's not really about grief but about change. The changes we didn't want to happen.

He says that there is a no-judgment zone when it comes to grief. Nothing like "This grief is worse than that one." Whatever has happened, whatever you are facing, whatever change has thrown your life off the track it was on—that is your grief. Comparison sends you down a dark road. You will always find someone who is "worse off" or "better off" than you.[2]

All of a sudden, this mourning announcement opens its arms and welcomes us all in.

Maybe you've been abused or raped, had a miscarriage or an abortion, experienced a divorce, a separation, or a friendship gone, been unfaithful and got found out, lost a career, sustained an injury, got diagnosed with cancer or convicted of a crime, sent your last child off to college. Things like these and more force us into surprising and unwanted transitions of some kind.

Unexpected change shifts the course of our lives, and there's grief in that.

We can also mourn what's never been. For instance, maybe we were abandoned and grew up without knowing a dad or a mum, or perhaps through happenstance we were born into poverty or an underprivileged or oppressed community. We are missing something that would have been there for us had our circumstances been different, and, locked deep inside us, a latent sadness waits to be unleashed.

Al Andrews is a wise sage, my counselor and spiritual director, an amazing listener, but best of all a great friend. He has this theory that there is a river of sorrow that flows through all of us deeply, and if we knew how to access it at any moment we would be sobbing messes.[3]

This deep sorrow is not a bad thing—in fact, it's really good. It's the sorrow of not being home or where we belong. The sorrow of being homesick. The sorrow of what our eyes have seen over the years.

The question is whether we are going to be willing to access this deep river of sorrow and find it—befriend it.

Al is often asked, "Why do we have to go there? You know it's past. It's done."

And Al always quotes the Beatitudes: "Because if you mourn, you will be comforted, and if you don't, you won't be."

And if you feel as though you don't have a reason to mourn or deserve to mourn or want to mourn? My friend Brad Nelson, a pastor and teacher in Florida, says,

The Greek word for "mourn" is *pentheo*. It refers to someone mourning the power of the wicked over the righteous. This is about the people who are at the bottom, those who feel trapped and helpless and are brokenhearted because of it. This is about the person who works three jobs but still can't make ends meet. It's about the parents who read all the parenting books and give their very best to a child who continues to make bad decisions. It's about the student who feels left out and misunderstood and mocked by classmates. It's about the little girl who has been forced into prostitution. In other words, there isn't any place in the human story you can look where you won't find a little *pentheo*. This is about all of us when we're helpless and trapped, brokenhearted and at the bottom.[4]

We all find ourselves there at times. Blessed are those who are helpless and trapped, brokenhearted and at rock bottom.

Welcome again to the upside-down message of the Beatitudes, where we find out that in the emptiness, when all hope seems lost, when we can't fix it, when we are grieving the absence of righteousness and justice, when there is no joy—

God is on our side.

EMBRACED

So what does "comfort" look like?

David Kessler is often told, "I'm trying to get rid of this grief, and I can't get rid of it. I'm trying to get past it, and I can't get past it." He says that the more we "try," the more we resist. The only way is to go through it. We have to feel the grief.[5]

And not only feel the grief but have someone around who sees us. The simple act of being seen gives us permission to grieve.

It's a hard thing—having your life so radically changed one day, and then the next day to see everyone else carrying on as if nothing has happened.

Does anyone see me? Does anybody care?

And maybe this is the heart of pain. We long for a witness. We long for people to see what we are going through. We long for someone to affirm the devastation. Because we weren't made to live alone. We were made for each other, and nothing separates us as quickly as pain we can't relate to.

The Golden Gate Bridge in San Francisco is the most famous place in the world where people commit suicide. One side of the bridge faces the Pacific. The other faces the city. Almost everyone who jumps, jumps from the city side. I wonder if they're looking for witnesses. And it doesn't take much imagination to hear their souls shouting, "There is no one to comfort me!" (see Lamentations 1:21) as they jump.

David Kessler shares a brilliant story about a village somewhere in the world, where if someone dies, all the households in the village change something in their own yard or on their house that very night. The next day, when those who are mourning leave their house, they not only know for themselves that their world has changed, but see that the world has changed and that things will not be the same for everyone around them too.

We should all have that tradition. The most healing we can offer is to let the pain of others disrupt us.

Shivah in the Jewish tradition is like this. *Shivah* literally means "seven" and signifies the seven days of mourning after a close family member dies and is buried. The family does something called "sitting shivah," where they receive visitors into the family home. It's an ancient ritual dating back to what Joseph did in Genesis when his father, Jacob, died. The purpose of the visit is to offer comfort, and that comfort comes sometimes without words. It's being there, it's seeing their grief, it's joining with them. It's being present.

This can unlock a piece of Jesus' baffling announcement about comfort to those who mourn, because in our pain and our grief, in the injustice of our circumstances, when we want answers in plain black and white, when we are angry, when we are crying out for clarity and a way to get past this grief, when we are in this dark, deafening, lonely silence—

We are offered *presence*, and God finds us in the places we are least likely to look.

I was recently listening to an NPR podcast where Martin Sheen, the actor, activist, and—as I found out—devout Catholic, shared his beautiful and inspiring spiritual journey:

Most of us, you know, will pray when . . . we are in the form of a crisis or we want something or we feel we need something. . . . I saw an interesting thing the other day in the paper. Somebody, one of the [presidential] candidates, was asked where God was when 9/11 happened, and he said, "Well, there's good and there's evil in the world, and we have to be aware of that." Well, my response to that would have been that God was in the towers. God was present to each individual going through that horrible—facing their own death individually and with a community. That God is present in our deepest hungers and our worst times as well as our best, but we often are forced to pray in ways that we can never articulate in bad times. How often the expression is "Oh my God" when we see something good or evil.[6]

We want answers. What is offered is *presence*.

WHAT DOES PRESENCE LOOK LIKE?

During our first week in our new home in Franklin, we came home to a note attached to the front door:

STU – 7 o'clock – Alright – Coffee – Cake – Jimmy, Carol, Scott

Jimmy, Carol, and Scott were our new neighbors. We weren't sure if the note was an invitation or an instruction, but, already stunned by the warmth and hospitality that we had been shown here in the South, we couldn't refuse.

When seven o'clock came, we knocked at the door and quickly learned that they were not from the South either. Jimmy was New York Italian (which explains the invitation) and had been married to Carol for nearly sixty years. They had moved to Tennessee to be close to family and grandchildren.

And so we got to know Jimmy, Carol, and their forty-something-year-old son, Scott. Scott has Down Syndrome, and he delighted in showing us family photos from the '80s and his taekwondo outfits emblazoned with all his achievements. It was a super fun time, and the coffee and cake were delicious!

For the next couple of years, we'd see Jimmy every day, working on the neighborhood landscape or mowing his lawn or spending time at the pool with his family. Scott, apart from being a black belt in taekwondo, was an amazing corn hole player and practiced for hours in the backyard with his imaginary friends and some marvelous and hilarious commentary.

Jimmy took it on himself to show us the neighborhood ropes, make sure we got to know everyone, and tell us everything we needed to know about the homeowners association, which was a new concept for us. In the UK, if we didn't cut our grass, we'd get long grass. If we don't cut our grass in our new neighborhood, we get a fifty-dollar fine.

One day, two years after moving in, we found out that Carol had cancer, and it was pretty clear that it was advanced and serious. After a few months of treatments so harsh and devastating on the body, it became all too much. Carol died in the spring of 2012.

Jimmy came and told us, a man not knowing how to handle his grief, voice wavering in shock at losing his wife of sixty years. Scott told us the best way he knew how, by coming over to Karen and me and holding us in his famous bear hug.

There were no words, really, to offer Jimmy. Everything I felt like saying seemed trite and shallow, but for us as friends and quite literally next-door neighbors, it didn't seem right to withdraw completely and let him get on with it just because I didn't know what to say.

It was April, and the spring weather was warming up fast like it had no regard for the fact that life had stopped for Jimmy and Scott. Nature sent a message from the divine; the trees were budding and the grass just kept growing, as if to say, "We have to carry on." So that was it. For the next few weeks, without being asked, my way of joining with Jimmy's pain and being present was to mow his lawn.

He never forgot it.

Jimmy turned eighty the year after, and losing his lifelong companion took its own toll. We watched Jimmy's health decline, and we watched his heart break. It seemed like his body decided that it was too much to bear, and after a series of strokes, Jimmy also passed, a year after Carol.

I don't know how this works—no one does—but I like to imagine their joy at being reunited.

Observing Jimmy's mourning and grief showed me that I, too, am in mourning for the things that have changed in my life. God is there in the pain and grief, no question.

That's the promise. That's the blessing. That's the presence.

We don't need answers; we need each other.

The ministry of presence. Compassion.

God cannot resist the cry of those who mourn. I'm reminded of what happened during the 400-meter semifinal at the 1992 Barcelona Olympics. Derek Redmond's dreams of gold fell apart when he tore his hamstring in front of millions of people. His dad fought his way onto the track to help his son across the finish line. He ran past the security. He chased the security off. Why? Because he couldn't resist the pain. He had to go to it. He had to share it. Because he knew, deep down, the pain was his, too.

Blessed are those who ache, for wherever they are, God is in their midst.

ALL GOOD THINGS MUST PASS

A few months ago we lost our dog, Buddy. He'd been with us nearly fourteen years.

He was a proud and beautiful standard schnauzer, part of

our family, and all of you who have dogs will know exactly what I mean. We got him at a time when we were deciding whether we were going to have another baby. In the end we decided that with me travelling so much with Delirious? and us living far away from our families and their help, our family was complete with our two beautiful daughters. But maybe we should get a puppy, as he would help Karen and the girls feel that little bit safer on those long, dark nights when I was away.

Little did we know what we were in for!

We used to walk Buddy along the West Sussex beach every day, but as much as we trained him and taught him to heel or never be out of our sight, if he saw a fox, a rabbit, a horse, or an unwitting jogger, he would disappear to protect us from whoever or whatever the oncoming "danger" was. So embarrassing!

It was not uncommon for one of our dog-owning friends (Buster's dad or Lucy's mum—you always know fellow dog walkers by their dogs' names!) to find Karen on the beach and say, "Have you lost Buddy? I think I just saw him chasing a fox along Dolphin Way!"

When it was time to move to Nashville, we got Buddy a pet passport (yes, there is such a thing), then flew him to Nashville and picked him up, a quivering wreck happy to be reunited with us and going to our new family home.

Buddy loved living in Nashville, although I think he missed the beach. He quickly decided that squirrels were his archenemy and delighted in chasing them up our flowering pear tree and standing guard, never really knowing if they were still up there hiding.

A couple of years ago he stopped jumping in or out of the car. We knew he was getting old, and with the onset of various ailments we decided that nothing was too good for our four-legged friend. We found the best veterinary help we could afford along the way.

But time catches up with all of us in the end, and after the last procedure to remove an ominous lump on his leg, he just couldn't recover. We had *that* call from the vet: "I think you should come in and decide what to do."

Thankfully it was a day that I was at home, and so Karen and I went into the dimly lit treatment room together at the animal hospital and said not just good-bye, but also thank you. Thank you for not only being a great dog, but being *our* dog. It still brings a lump to my throat now.

I was with my friend Ian Cron one day when he had to go and do the same thing with his dog, Hobbs. We talked at length about what it means to be a good steward of the animals we have in our lives. When Buddy died, Ian sent me a message that was something like this: *So sorry, such a bummer! I think it's often as hard to say good-bye to dogs as it is to people. Prayers and love to you and Karen.*

Another message I got was from my friend Jimmy Abegg. Jimmy was one of Rich Mullins's Ragamuffins:

Hey Stu . . . Woke up thinking about you guys today. Michelle told me last night about you losing Buddy. Sure sorry to hear about him. All good things must pass. I woke up today also thinking about losing Rich [Mullins] eighteen years ago in a couple of days. Wow, where does the time go?

Buddy taught us a lot in his final moments, and Ian and Jimmy offered their *presence*.

We mourn our loss of Buddy, but maybe there's more. Maybe

we mourn the baby we never had too. There's more than one grief lurking beneath the surface, waiting to be awakened by another triggered change.

So while the wound is as vast as the sea and we mourn loved ones lost, as we detach from careers ending, as we ache in the absence of something we once had or that we never had, we, too, can grieve loss.

And just like in the grass in spring, we discover the invitation to carry on.

MEEK

When Presence Is Ignored

The meek may inherit the earth,
but they won't get the ball from me.

CHARLES BARKLEY

• • •

Blessed are the meek,
for they will inherit the earth.

MATTHEW 5:5

• • •

You're blessed when you're content with just
who you are—no more, no less. That's the
moment you find yourselves proud owners
of everything that can't be bought.

MATTHEW 5:5, MSG

• • •

I will be higher than a mother
Safer than a place to hide
I will be more than just your shelter
I will be your home

"I WILL BE YOUR HOME (MEEK),"
AUDREY ASSAD AND STU G

WHO GETS THE EARTH?

Because *that* is the question on all of our lips, right?
I think we all know who gets the earth!

- the successful, the strong, the brutal, the bullies
- those who climb their way to the top
- those who sell the most books
- those with the most Facebook friends
- those with the most Apple products (I have four)
- those whose frequent-flier card says "Executive Platinum" (mine says "Platinum" . . . boo!)

And then my guess is, if you've grown up like me, you have something like this as an understanding of what *meek* means:

- the humble
- the wallflowers
- those who don't correct you when you say their name wrong
- those who don't fight for their place in line when someone pushes in front
- those who stand by and watch others get ahead
- those who get walked on . . . the doormats
- the "sat upon, spat upon, ratted on"[1]

The "little people" don't inherit the earth. The big, aggressive ones do.

I have to admit I've got power problems. You might not notice them at first, because they are well camouflaged, but they're there, tucked away, ready to pounce and grab when anything I want comes my way.

I remember back in the day, whenever a generous manufacturer would send us boys in Delirious? a box of free goodies—designer T-shirts and sunglasses, some kind of free swag that could make me look cool—there was always that irritating urge to get to the box first, and if I didn't, I had that terrible feeling of missing out on the best piece.

I hate that feeling of being left out or passed over. I've had to battle that feeling of entitlement. My gut reaction is to want to get to the front first, stick a flag in the ground, and stake my claim.

So who are the meek?

Maybe we should look around the hillside that day. Jesus didn't announce these things for the benefit of people who weren't there. He was speaking to the very people who needed to hear what he had to say.

And there was quite a crowd. We only have Matthew's words and not any iPhone footage, but at the end of Matthew 4, which many scholars read as the setup for the sermon, Matthew says that Jesus had been going out and getting among the people where they lived, teaching the truth of God's Kingdom, and healing peoples' bodies *and* minds—and these people followed him. The NIV says that "large crowds" came from Galilee (a very Jewish area where Jesus grew up), the Ten Towns or Decapolis (a Greek area settled by Alexander the Great), Jerusalem, Judea, and the area across the Jordan.

Matthew is showing us that the people following Jesus were from all over the region, all the points of the compass. It was a ragtag jumble of people and culture.

Jesus' message is that *all* are included. Even the ones outside our religion and prejudices. All these people's lives had been touched by this travelling teacher, living proof that once you've experienced love and hope and mercy, it's hard to stay away.

Love, hope, and mercy were a rare commodity in a land occupied by the Roman superpower that was in charge from the British Channel to Asia Minor. These people had lost their homes and land and families. They were broken and trampled upon. The middle classes had disappeared because of high taxes, and all that were left were the very rich (the colluders) or the very poor (everyone else).

These are Matthew's meek, his "little people":

- those who are overpowered and oppressed
- those who are bullied and marginalized
- those who have lost the power of choice and opportunity
- those who are born into the "wrong" family or religious community
- those who are seen as "the other" or "the outsider"

This beatitude is for those in awful situations who lack the power to do anything about it. This is about a poverty of power and choice. It's about the ones who, with great humility, hear and accept the invitation to find a way to carry on in the most awful, difficult, and dire circumstances.

The invitation to carry on comes from a man who came not to overthrow with violence and revenge and entitlement, but to lead the way in nonviolence. Showing us how to love our enemies. Healing our bodies and minds. It's a hard, countercultural, upside-down message to hear—especially when you are being violated, and you just want to punch some faces . . . or rise up and over-throw your oppressor with force and revenge.

In fact, I think in part this beatitude is a messianic political statement. If there was a large gathering, I'm sure there were Romans present, representatives of the superpower, making sure things didn't get out of hand. I can imagine a note of defiance in our Teacher's voice as he said that the little people are the ones who will get the earth.

WHO ARE THE TWENTY-FIRST-CENTURY MEEK?

I don't mean for this to sound patronizing, but all we have to do is open our eyes. The invitation to look around the hillside in Galilee two thousand years ago is the invitation to look around us today, wherever we are. The meek are in our towns and cities, but they remain unnoticed and will stay unseen unless we take the time to look and be present, become friends and share our lives.

A definition I've come to use a lot is that the meek are those whose presence is constantly denied or ignored. They are not just powerless. Power has never been an option.

It's so easy to remain unseeing because these people are different from us—they might not believe the same stuff as we do. To engage will mean stepping outside our comfort zones to even be present to them.

I'm talking to myself.

I know what it's like to use all my time and energy to look after my family and try to keep my own head above water, so no bullying from me, but lately I've just felt a different kind of pull.

When I look at the story of Jesus and the message of the Beatitudes, I'm struck by how confronting it is to my comfort level. I really have to fight the feelings of trying to attain something or of not "doing" enough. The temptation to keep measuring myself against others who "do" awesome things is always with me, but it's such a distraction. It's so easy to fall into ways of attaining, which completely misses the point. This is about who we are and not what we do; it's about being and not doing.

I look at Jesus, who said,

> Are you tired? Worn out? Burned out on religion? Come to me. Get away with me and you'll recover your life. I'll show you how to take a real rest. Walk with me and work with me—watch how I do it. Learn the unforced rhythms of grace. I won't lay anything heavy or ill-fitting on you. Keep company with me and you'll learn to live freely and lightly.
>
> MATTHEW 11:28-30, MSG

"Watch how I do it."
Whom did he have meals with? Whom did he spend time with?

- a tax collector, despised by most people
- a prostitute
- a Roman centurion
- the poor and needy
- the wealthy and envied
- the lepers
- the demon-possessed

So many people shut out by religion, society, and the righteous.

So I've been stepping out of my comfort zone and reaching

out to make new friends around me where I live and move right now. I'm feeling the pull to "learn the unforced rhythms of grace." I'm beginning to open my eyes and open myself to the community around me, and I'm starting to notice those who are different from me, those who haven't chosen their life or circumstances. Those who are meek because they are "the other."

I feel so up against the ropes here because each person and the group they represent could have a whole book written about them. This is such a personal journey, and in some ways it feels so small to me. I know I have blind spots, and there are a ton of folks missing from this chapter—for instance, the elderly, the disabled, and the homeless. But the people I introduce to you here are folks that I am beginning to form genuine connections with. They are *my* people in *my* city. And I hope that as you read, you will be inspired to look around your own towns and cities, because the meek are always around us.

THE MARGINALIZED

Swapping life in the south of England for a life in the southern United States brought huge challenges for us—mostly emotional ones, along with some cultural differences. But making this change in white British skin means that ours is a different and privileged story compared to those of some folks who were born here.

Every day on my way to the studio in downtown Franklin, I would drive past Natchez Street. On the corner is a church called First Missionary Baptist. It's in a low-income neighborhood, mostly public housing, and the residents are predominantly African American.

As I was driving past Natchez one particularly cold and frosty morning, I saw an elderly African American lady slip and hurt her head and face. Where I'm from, if you see that, you stop and help. So I did. I noticed a surprised look on the faces of neighbours as they came out to see if she was okay. I could see that her nose was broken, so I offered to take her to hospital. The folks around were really grateful but also seemed a bit taken aback. It must have been the accent, I thought.

It didn't even cross my mind that it might be because I had white skin.

Through our church community at Church of the City Franklin, I met Scott Roley, a white American guy a little older than me. When Scott was eleven years old, he stood in front of the Lincoln Memorial and heard Martin Luther King Jr. deliver his "I have a dream" speech. Pretty amazing, eh? Legendary!

Scott and his wife have been pouring their lives into racial reconciliation and income equality here in Franklin for thirty years. They live in a low-income, African American neighbourhood called Hard Bargain, where, Scott says, "the tough times that poverty dispenses heap up at your door."[2] They also attend First Missionary Baptist.

You'll hear more of Scott and his story later on in the book, but I can't begin to tell you the impact he and his work are having on me. He has opened up his life to us in such a generous and beautiful way.

Thanks to Scott's introduction, I go to a weekly Bible study meeting called The Empty Hands Fellowship at First Missionary Baptist, whenever the schedule allows. And I've made friends with some extraordinary people. Take Anthony Pickett, for example.

Anthony invited Karen and me to church after my first time at Bible study. We had never been to an African American church before and honestly didn't know what to expect. Just before 11:00 a.m. on Sunday morning, Anthony met us in the car park, grinning like he was surprised we showed up.

What we experienced was one of the greatest Sunday mornings we've ever had. I don't know that we've ever been made to feel more welcome in any church—anywhere—ever. Everything from the exuberant greetings, to the music and singing, to the extraordinary preaching was like a first-time experience. A day we'll never forget.

That was really our introduction into the African American world here in Franklin.

Trouble is, the pristine suits and dresses and hairstyles of a Sunday tell a different story from the low-income housing, the lack of jobs and opportunity, the poverty, and the struggle of the rest of the week.

Scott, the champion that he is, has been driving me around neighborhoods and introducing me to some people who've graciously agreed to share their stories of what life is like as a minority—as the meek—today.

Tangie Lane

Tangie Lane is a young, African American, married mother of two daughters. I've been struck by her wisdom. The struggle and oppression for her and her family is real. She's lived long enough to not simply get upset by it all but is making decisions constantly about whether to push back—because the discrimination she faces happens every day.

Her earliest memories of struggle were in first grade, with the girls she played with at school:

We were best friends, but I was never invited to any of their parties or sleepovers because their parents wouldn't allow it. My mom was so great and never sowed a seed of hatred. She showed her pain and allowed me to feel mine. She just said that some people think that just because other people look different, they *are* different. I never felt I had to choose a side. I am who I am, they are who they are, and we gotta learn how to work and live together. She was a great model for me.[3]

In high school, whenever racial tension bubbled up in the community, other students would put pictures of monkeys on the hallway walls, next to signs that told the African American students to go back to Africa.

The fact that our basketball team was the Franklin Rebels and the Confederate flag was the flag that was waved at our pep rallies—that was horrific. There were a bunch of students that tried to get that changed, but they were shut down. We would get told, "You're just mad, calm down, it's been this way forever."

But when outsiders started coming in, it helped with the change. People were horrified that the Confederate flag was getting run around at the rallies—and they thought we were okay with it. We weren't, but we couldn't get heard.

To Tangie, the flag really does represent the white suprema-cist movement and Ku Klux Klan racism. So when people say it's nothing, it's just history, that history reminds Tangie and her family of hangings, rapes, and lynchings.

I have to pause for a moment because I realize this is in my lifetime. The last officially recorded lynching in the United States was in 1981.[4] And there have been several Klan-style mur-ders since. The last recorded cross-burning incident in Franklin was 2002! Tangie said, "Even now with Black Lives Matter, the people that oppose that are still waving that flag. It's contradic-tory to what we are saying because Black Lives Matter does not mean that white lives don't matter! There're so many people that think that's what we're implying, but it's not. We are saying we're here, see us, we matter! It's not that you don't."

At home, Tangie and her husband spend time with their kids and tell the stories of their past. It's important to talk about it. They watch movies and then discuss them and so learn about African American history. Their girls are still young enough to say, "It's all changed now, Mom," but Tangie remembers being like that with her mother too. So she tells them that not everyone is out to get them, but they will still face certain per-ceptions and experiences as young black women.

Day-to-day discrimination is more noticeable for Tangie's husband, who is a tall basketball coach. In the grocery store, for instance, white people are often wary of his presence. If the kids are with him, less so, but most of the time people look at him as if he's going to mug them. As a black male, he's a regular target for profiling from the predominantly white police forces. This is why Black Lives Matter is so important. Things need to change. Tangie told me,

Before we were married my husband was driving in his car one night when a lady called the police saying she saw a black guy in a car holding a gun. The police pulled my husband over, and—before they asked him anything, before they did anything—my husband looked up, and there was a gun pointing at his head. It's things like this that the white majority never has to deal with.

When people of color break the law, they need to be arrested and face their punishment, but to make the assumption that someone is bad just by the way they look—and when things happen like what happened to Trayvon Martin, Michael Brown, Alton Sterling, and Philando Castile—it breaks my heart.

For Tangie it's usually while shopping that the subtle forms of discrimination show themselves: being passed over at a checkout, older white women expecting her to move out of their way. That's how they grew up too—unspoken rules of segregation passed down from generation to generation. For Tangie, being one of the meek literally looks like being ignored and treated like she's not there. "You just get tired of it because it happens over and over and over again," Tangie said, "and there comes a point when you just want to get angry."

Tangie shared how this unspoken segregation impacted a tragic season of their lives. She and her husband were expecting twins when the babies were born ten weeks premature. Devastatingly, the boy was stillborn. The girl had some brain trauma and eye problems and needed surgeries.

And as the days and weeks went on, Tangie wasn't feeling well. She said,

I knew there was something wrong. I called the doctor several times—but I was young, I was black, I was on Medicaid, and those things factored. There was this feeling like, "You shouldn't have been pregnant anyway." They couldn't figure out what was wrong with me. I nearly died as a result.

I filed a lawsuit against my doctor for negligence [in my son's death]. When determining how much money to ask for, my attorney explained that there is a formula that determines the amount you can sue for based on the deceased's (in my case, my unborn son's) race and earning potential—which ultimately means that this "formula" is based upon how most black men fare in society. Therefore, a mother of a white male could sue for a greater amount for the death of her unborn son, due to his race. It was like the system has its own league table of life—with white people at the top, the minorities further down the list, black males at the bottom. This was in the '90s.

When I ask Tangie what life is like now and the ways she is active in working for racial equality, she doesn't hesitate when she tells me, "Through education." Tangie works at New Hope Academy in Franklin as a teacher's assistant, investing in students just as teachers invested in her, giving her the opportunity to get a degree and have more choices in the life she has today. She believes that education changes everything, providing opportunities and choices. She's working with kids who could fall through the gaps: They come from low-income families, some of them broken families, some of them with parents in jail. She is working to break the stigma and cycle of inequality. Tangie uses her own story to intentionally disrupt the stories of these bright, beautiful kids by being a messenger and bringer of hope.

Every day, Tangie finds the strength to stay on the path of seeking equality and justice, of fighting for love and not hate.

Charles Robinson

Charles Robinson is a member of the Choctaw tribe of Oklahoma. I met with him because I was fascinated to learn about the first people to live on this land. You don't see much evidence around where we live that they were ever here, and he tells me that actually it's unique being a Native American here in Middle Tennessee because not many are around. His wife, Siouxsan, is part Lakota and part Blackfoot; she often gets mistaken for someone of Hispanic descent, and that means she sometimes faces discrimination such as staff following her around Walmart, making sure she's not stealing anything.

When folks meet Charles and find out he's Choctaw, they want to talk about *Dances with Wolves* and how they have Native blood in their family, but when Charles teaches folks of the hardship and the terrible treatment his people have faced, everyone is shocked. "We didn't know that," they say, because it's a story that's not taught in schools. No one wants to take responsibility.

Most of the time Charles is not offended when people call him "Chief" or "Injun Joe" or "redskin," because they don't realize what they are saying or the history behind it. People use phrases that they have no idea could be racist or offensive. Charles says we have not been taught the history, so we have no idea.[5]

So I asked Charles to give me a brief history lesson.

The U.S. government recognizes 566 different tribes.[6]

There are about 175 tribal languages still spoken.[7]

Pre-1492 (the date when Western Europeans landed in the Americas), the population of Native people in what we now call the United States was somewhere between 1.5 and 10 million. By 1900, there were only about 237,000 Native people.[8] Basically, in four hundred years, Native Americans were almost wiped out by Western Europeans.

In 1830 President Andrew Jackson signed the "Indian Removal Act," which moved thousands of Native Americans to Oklahoma. Jackson actually met with the Chickasaw right here in Franklin. Tens of thousands of people had to leave with whatever they could gather and carry or—if they were lucky—put in a carriage. Many thousands of people died on what became known as the Trail of Tears. The Choctaw, who were removed from Alabama and Louisiana, have special burial traditions. When many of them died on the Trail of Tears, survivors were not allowed to grieve and mourn their dead with a traditional burial.

Charles told me about the more recent history of boarding schools or residential schools that Native children had to go through for generations—even Charles's own mother. They had to cut their hair and weren't allowed to speak their language or carry on with their traditions. The sexual and physical and emotional abuse was terrible. The children were forced to assimilate into white culture and often felt ashamed of the color of their skin.

The oppression and abuse of these peoples is stunning. And most of us don't know a thing about it.

So when I use *meek* as a term to describe the Native American people, it's because their suffering and oppression, their human rights—and in fact their very presence—have been constantly ignored for many generations. It's not surprising that problems have emerged within their communities.

Charles explained to me that the stereotypical problems we see the Native American population facing—the abuses of drugs and alcohol; physical, mental, sexual, and emotional abuse; school drop-outs; obesity; and a rejection of traditional values—really come from this feeling of hopelessness that is passed down through the generations. Addiction rates are between four and six times the national average, suicide rates are seven times the national average, unemployment is at 80 to 85 percent—and only 3 to 5 percent of the population say they are Christians because much of the historic damage has been done by people who represented the church.

Having said that, Charles, a Choctaw, is also a Jesus follower. He started something called The Red Road, a nonprofit that helps other organizations connect to Native Americans and educates people on the lives of Native Americans. He is passionate about taking the time to get to know someone, and that's something the dominant culture hasn't done with Native Americans. He is urging us to take the time to learn the story so that these people don't become faceless and nameless.

"To walk the red road" is a familiar term to Native Americans. It kind of means to live an unbroken lifestyle. So Charles is promoting living a traditional lifestyle: no addiction to drugs or alcohol, respect for others and for yourself, respect for creation, and worship of the Creator.

What Charles offers is fascinating. Something that is honoring to Native culture and also honoring to churches and ministries who work on the reservations. Oftentimes these are run by non-Natives and aren't always well received, so Charles comes alongside the work that others are doing and validates and builds bridges.

The Red Road also does something called Baskets of Hope, which are laundry baskets filled with about a hundred dollars' worth of household goods:

> We go and we give them to households on the reservations. Sometimes it's just a gift and they shut the door; sometimes they invite us in for coffee. That way we can begin to become friends, get to know them, and help with their spiritual needs. The funny thing is when you talk about what Jesus taught in terms of loving your neighbor, looking after the poor, the widow, clothing the naked, visiting the prisoner—it lines up alongside what the Natives believe. So we don't say we're Christians. We say we're following the teaching of Jesus.

Hundreds of years of oppression, marginalization, being used, being ignored, and not having a voice is what being meek looks like for many Native Americans and African Americans. The Beatitudes announce that these people matter—their culture, their history, their centuries of pain matter. May we open our hearts and eyes to see and be present to those who are promised the earth.

THE DISPLACED

My heart hurts for those on the planet right now displaced by war and violence. It's impossible to avoid the news of the current refugee and migration crisis.

I'm convinced these people are some of the twenty-first-century meek. Literally fleeing their homes, their friends, their communities with whatever they can carry in a few bags. Losing their life savings to escape persecution. I ache for this injustice to end and I long for peace. We cannot turn a blind eye to these hurting people.

In 2015 we watched the plight of over one million refugees and migrants flooding into Europe, some fleeing ISIS in Iraq and Syria but also conflict, poverty, and abuse in Afghanistan, Kosovo, Albania, Pakistan, Eritrea, Nigeria, Serbia, and Ukraine.

As I sit here in Tennessee, it is impossible to get my head around the fact that in 2015, 12.4 million people were newly displaced, forced to leave their homes due to conflict and persecution. That's twenty-four people every minute.[9]

Unbelievable.

It's all so far away.

Diving into news channels on YouTube, I came across a piece from the *Guardian UK*, reporting from Jordan at the Zaatari Syrian refugee camp. A young mother, who has seen and fled from more than we can imagine, said this: "It's a difficult feeling, when a mother feels that she has to defend her children. Very often a man cannot defend himself, his children or anyone. One has to work against reality. A mother must be higher than a mother, stronger than a mother."[10]

How does a mother be more than a mother? Higher than a mother? I cried as I watched.

Fady Al-Hagal

I recently met a man called Fady Al-Hagal. Fady is Syrian and left his family home thirtysomething years ago to go to college in Tennessee. He wasn't a refugee but knew only four words of English when he arrived: *hi, good-bye, yes*, and *no*. He tells a hilarious but poignant story of meeting the immigration officer when he arrived in New York. It went something like this:

Officer: Where are you coming from?
Fady: Hi.
Officer (motioning to the bench): Open your suitcase.
Fady: Good-bye.
Officer: No, no—open your suitcase!

The officer grabbed the suitcase and put it on the bench.

Officer: Give me the key.
Fady: [blank look][11]

Realizing there was a language barrier, the officer motioned for the key and then opened the suitcase . . . and found a bag of white powder sitting at the top. Now, it was actually some Middle Eastern cooking powder, but the officer thought it was cocaine, and the scene turned to chaos as other officers came over to investigate. Once they tested the powder and discovered it was in fact *not* cocaine, the officer stamped Fady's documents and sent him on his way.

Fady had no idea where to go or what to do—he just had his luggage and tickets for the next flight to Memphis. He wandered out to try to find his way and got caught walking against the flow of travelers. A uniformed airport official was telling Fady to "move, move, move," but of course, not understanding the language, Fady thought he was in trouble. The airport official grabbed his tickets and noticed that Fady had only fifty minutes to make his next flight from LaGuardia. And, as it turned out, he had arrived in JFK.

The uniformed airport official took Fady by the arm and put him in a taxi. Fady thought he was going to jail. The chaos continued at LaGuardia, but Fady made his flight. Once on the plane he took his seat next to a drunk guy who asked him, "Do you like Kenny Rogers?"

Remember, Fady knew only four words of English. So he said, "Yes," and for the next two hours this guy sang Kenny Rogers songs to Fady, all the time breathing whiskey fumes.

Fady got to Martin, Tennessee, completed his education, and ended up staying, getting married, and becoming a U.S. citizen. He now works for the brilliant nongovernmental organization World Relief and is working on a program to help refugees settle in Nashville. It's a huge task!

Fady tells his immigration story to highlight something of what it's like for the refugees he works with. How on arrival it's scary, emotional, frustrating—how you wonder if you are ever going to make it. No familiar faces, no familiar voices. You are the stranger that nobody understands and everybody ignores— and now, everybody is afraid of.

Fady explained that refugees not only have just lost their homes, escaping injury or certain death, but may have endured a perilous journey with smugglers or risked their lives on a boat across the Mediterranean. They then have to prove that they qualify for refugee status by showing that they were persecuted or fear persecution due to race, religion, nationality, political opinion, or their membership in a particular social group.

When you become a refugee, you become "stateless"—usually

in a refugee camp or holding centre of some kind. It's completely disorienting and chaotic, and there is so much unknown. All you want to do is go back to your home and live in peace. Going back home is the hope of every refugee.

In Syria alone, 11 million people have been uprooted and displaced by the war, and 300,000 have been killed.[12]

It can take months or years before refugees know where they will be settled. I heard of one Syrian family who waited in Jordan for almost two years, hoping to go to Sweden, only to find that Sweden would not accept any more refugees. Next they were told they were going to Finland; then that was cancelled. With very little notice, they were told America was their destination, and they gathered their things in a hurry to be on their way.[13]

This young family was settled in Dallas, Texas, and the father got a job stocking shelves on the midnight shift at his local Walmart. A far cry from his job at a health care company in Syria, but as any father would do, he did whatever it took to provide for his family.

Then the terror attacks happened in Paris, and the backlash started. The House of Representatives voted to tighten the oversight of refugees coming into the country. Governors objected to refugees being settled in their states. Presidential candidates swore to have refugees deported.[14] Intimidating, to say the least.

The process for refugees entering the country is already "the most rigorous screening and security vetting of any category of traveler to the United States."[15] And only about 50 percent of the refugees that the United Nations presents to the United States for resettlement are considered.

All this family wanted was to escape violence and get on with their lives, and they are some of the "lucky" ones, grateful that, even despite potential racist backlash, they have found America to be a place of hope and opportunity, a place to build a future. Sometimes the meek look like the disoriented stranger that nobody understands and everybody is afraid of.

THE OTHER

Being the other is incredibly lonely. It means you—like so many of these meek we've talked about—are ignored, overlooked, dismissed, distrusted. You're different, you're the outsider—and it feels like you have no one on your side. The surprising, counterintuitive—countercultural even—message of the Beatitudes is that when this is your life and experience, Jesus announces, "You are blessed. God is on your side."

Riyad and James are two friends with hard stories—they have vastly different experiences and backgrounds, but the common ground of being "the other" in our American society. And as we've become friends, they have taught me a lot about what it means to be meek.

Riyad Al-Kasem

We have lived here in Tennessee for several years now and have really focused our time on finding our way—making a living and creating a new home as a family. All good stuff, but after meeting Fady and hearing stories of refugees, I realized I had no friends who are part of the Muslim community. I wanted to do something about that. I really wanted to meet someone, a religious Muslim, and find out what it's like to live here, in America in the southern states, post-9/11 and in the age of ISIS.

I had heard of the Islamic Center of Nashville (I'd inadvertently parked in their car park by mistake once), so I looked on their website and e-mailed the PR representative, explaining what I am doing with The Beatitudes Project and this book and asking if there was someone I could meet and talk with. Riyad hit me back straightaway, and his story was eye-opening.

On a beautiful September morning in Santa Barbara, California, Riyad Al-Kasem woke up to hear the devastating news of the attacks on the Twin Towers at the World Trade Center in New York. Within an hour he received a death threat.

Riyad had moved to America from Syria a few years previously, after graduating law school with flying colors. During his time at law school, Riyad's professor had encouraged him to study the laws and governments of other countries around the world, and what he discovered changed his life. He began to think that maybe the Assad socialist regime wasn't the pinnacle of government, as was taught in school.

Riyad was particularly impressed when he learned of the "checks and balances" system of the United States, where even the leader of the country is held accountable by the law. *This is the kind of country I want to live in*, he thought.

His thesis reached Syrian government eyes and ears, and the secret service visited the family home, asking his father if Riyad would change his views on the government and the future of the country.[16]

Riyad wasn't going to change his views or keep quiet about them anytime soon, so he decided to leave Syria rather than put his family in danger. He left his hopes for a future in the justice system in Syria, moved to California, and began washing dishes as a way to make ends meet.

He met his American wife and became a citizen, and they

had two sons and a happy family life in Santa Barbara. On July 4, 2001, his mother visited from Syria and was fascinated by the holiday. She asked how they celebrated Independence Day and wanted her own American flag. They waved their flags, joined the neighbors' parties. Riyad was so proud, felt fully at home, and finally belonged to this great country of America.

And then, on that fateful day in September, everything changed.

"We became the other, the outsiders, the ones to be suspicious of," Riyad told me.

What was most worrying was how life was changing for his sons. A racist neighbor chased Riyad's four-year-old son across his yard with a hunting knife, calling the petrified boy "raghead" and screaming at him to "go back home." Confused and distraught, the boy asked his mother, "What did he mean 'go home'? Where is home?"

The next day the same neighbor was polishing his semi-automatic machine gun, while wearing full camo gear, in front of Riyad's home. Riyad's son is now twenty-one years old. He is still haunted by that day.

It wasn't all a nightmare. The Christian and Jewish communities immediately started reaching out to the Islamic community in California, showing Riyad and his friends that they just had to "keep reaching out and show that true Islam is a peaceful religion."

Since 9/11, the genesis of ISIS, the Paris and Belgium attacks, the massacre in Orlando, and ISIS's continued efforts to create unrest and terror around the world, the Muslim community is increasingly viewed with suspicion and fear. And it's clear that because of that fear, kind and peaceful people—many of them fleeing terror and violence themselves—are increasingly being marginalized, not just in America but around the world.

There is so much polarization in the world right now, especially where politics and religion are concerned, and the Internet really doesn't help, does it? So rather than learn about Islam from fearful gut reactions on Facebook, I decided I wanted to learn about Islam from my neighbors.

On the hottest winter day since records began, I left the Nashville skyline fading into the distance behind me and headed out to the town of Hendersonville, to Café Rakka, the restaurant that Riyad and his wife opened after moving to Tennessee from California. For five generations Riyad's family have been known for their butter, cheese, and yoghurt making. An uncle taught Riyad how to cook, and Café Rakka is the result of his passion for cooking. The food is deliciously amazing—Syrian, Mediterranean, and Silk Road flavors combining in a delightful way.

I walked in past a guy tucking into a lunch of falafel and salad. He was wearing a Donald Trump hat. "I don't know what he believes, but he loves my food," Riyad said later, laughing. "The eggplant or shawarma and falafel are not gonna take any side, so neither am I. I'm building bridges with my food."

And building bridges is what Riyad does every day. He is clear on this. If anyone is fearful, he can help change fear into friendship. But if some people have already decided that they are going to hate him, there's not a lot he can do with that.

As an active member of the community at the Islamic Center of Nashville, Riyad sees interfaith work and dialogue as his personal mission. And building relationships is vitally important for a better future.

Riyad has become a good friend. He and his community are trying so hard to get back to what it was like on July 4, 2001. "All we can do," he says, "is give 100 percent effort. Maybe it will take another generation, but we have to start right now so our kids cannot say, 'Why didn't you try?'"

James Grady

James is a Jew. He's a part of the West End Synagogue in Nashville. He's an academic with an MA in philosophy and religion. And we had an awesome conversation about what it was like for him to grow up outside the Christian tradition in the southern United States.[17]

It may sound a strange thing for us to talk about, but if you spent time here in Nashville, I think you'd understand. There are over nine hundred churches in the greater Nashville area. Sometimes they're next to each other on the street. It's quite extraordinary. When we moved here, our neighbors didn't necessarily ask, "Would you like to come round for dinner?" or "Shall we go to the pub?" They asked, "Would you like to come to our church?"

It took a little while to get used to this atmosphere of religion in the Bible Belt. (For the sake of non-Americans reading this, the Bible Belt runs all the way across the southeastern and south central states, from Florida to Texas.) The evangelical church is strong here, culturally and politically. This is a broad stroke, but historically it's not always been kind and accepting to groups it doesn't agree with.

To that point, James is also part of the LGBT community. James is editor of *Out & About Nashville* magazine and advocates for the rights of LGBT people across the state and beyond because—as I've found out—the system of state law is also at times not kind and accepting of this community. I'm so glad James responded to my request to chat. Some other LGBT folks had not felt so comfortable in being vulnerable with their stories because I'm writing this book as a Christian, as a follower of Jesus. And the LGBT community finds Christians hard to trust sometimes.

I want to say right off the bat that what I'm offering to you here is about our neighbors. Those among us who are marginalized and bullied and seen as "the other." I'm not talking about theological or political correctness. It's about "Who is my neighbor?" It's about how we see each other, how we treat each other—it's about our fellow human beings, who carry the image of God. I'm not asking anyone to change their theology. I'm asking us to consider what James, like the others in this chapter, may have to teach us about being meek, being seen as different, and being discriminated against. And I'm challenging us to widen our circle of friends and get to know people who are different from us.

I'm not sure the Beatitudes point us toward tolerance. Plus, I'm not sure I really like that word—it implies that I'm simply "putting up" with you. Rather, I think our Teacher is pointing us toward engagement and kindness—justice and mercy. Pointing us toward common ground, which starts with presence in our brokenness. God sees you—so I see you. I hope you see me, too.

Our society and communities are so polarized. If we come at this conversation with a position of pride and certainty, we just polarize even further.[18]

James grew up in Dalton, Georgia, and lived most of the time with his great-grandmother, who was Southern Baptist. He says some things matter here in the South that you can't even imagine mattering anywhere else. It was common even in school for a stranger to come up and ask, "Are you saved?" Which, when you think about it, is weird.

I remember going to Vacation Bible School one summer, and when everyone else was released to go to their grades, all the kids who were over nine were forced to stay in the auditorium. The minister came in and basically was like, "It's time for you all to either be saved, or . . ." So basically it was like a show of hands—who all has been baptized? All of those kids were released. Then it was all the unbaptized children who were left, and the minister was basically like, "Hellfire and brimstone awaits you. You can die anytime!" Some of the compliant children started to get saved. There were maybe twenty people in the room. As he kept going, of course more kids got saved, and after a certain period of time the only people left were me and this Hispanic kid who was Catholic. He had just come with his friend. You know Catholics don't get saved, right? Catholics get baptized! So he and I were the only ones sitting there, and everyone else was in this ecstatic moment, and clearly the expectation was that we would get with the program. We did not get with the program.

James was interested in Christianity on an intellectual level, but "We need to save you" and "We need to fix you" felt invasive and like bullying to him. So James decided to follow the path of the Jewish side of his family.

We talked about this, because from my conversations with

my friend Rabbi Joseph I know that a lot of Jews in America grow up having to deal with incredible bullying. Not only did they "not recognize the Messiah," but they "killed him." When Rabbi Joseph was seven years old, he often rode his bike down the road to go play with his friends. But one day his friend answered the door and said, "Nope. You're a Christ killer." Joseph says that what he experienced that day—and what he continued to experience growing up—was the rejection of who he was. He became "the other."

James said he got so fed up with people asking if he was "saved" that in school there came a time when he started to take lunch to the library. And the bullies just followed him there.

When I was in eighth grade, someone put a knife to my neck on a school bus for forty-five minutes. In middle school, this very effeminate boy in my PE class was getting bullied, and I tried to stand up to the bully. From then on it was, "Is he your boyfriend?" I started to change for PE in the handicap bathrooms because they had locks. When I was a freshman in high school a group of boys on the bus would grab me or taunt me by making sexual suggestions. Then it moved into the halls at school.

Most members of the LGBT community hate anything to do with religion because of how they've been treated. James told me that although the LGBT community is less than 10 percent of the population, 40 percent of homeless youth between the ages of eighteen and twenty-four identify as LGBT. Many of them are on the streets because their lifestyle and their family's religion did not mix. We Christians feel like we have to "fix" people.

But our primary calling is to love them as we love ourselves (Matthew 22:39).

If we believe Jesus is the way, then we need to look at how he lived and moved. And Jesus went out to the marginalized and the bullied, the leper, the prostitute, the tax collector—people who were seen as "the other"—and said, "You matter, you're included—God is on your side!"

If I, as a white British guy, had been on the hill that day, I would have been "the other."

As I talked to James about this idea of meekness in regards to those who are marginalized and bullied, he turned the tables on me.

Are we by nature meek, or are we by necessity meek? Is it meekness not to talk about your experience because no one's listening, or is that just enforced meekness? Does it make a difference? I don't know if it makes a difference, but if we praise meekness as a virtue, then it does make a difference, right?

There's this certain way of taking the Beatitudes: "Oh, you're poor—that's the opportunity that God has given you! So stay poor!" or "You're coming in last right now, but don't worry about it, you'll be first in the Kingdom of Heaven." It can be used to justify people's suffering.

So I explained that in my understanding of the context of the Beatitudes, I don't think being meek is a virtue, and certainly not a way to justify people's suffering. It's about lack of power and choice. It doesn't mean that you're not strong or that you're not angry. You might be powerless to do anything about your situation, and if you do, if you fight back now, you might die or make it worse for your family. The meek are those who've had the power of choice and equality stripped away from them, but they find a way to carry on. They hear an invitation to another way of living.

This is what we learn from all these stories, all these people who are the twenty-first-century meek. The meek learn how to live with humility—but it isn't just subservience. The classic way Jesus framed this was when he talked about turning the other cheek so that the person has to hit you again. Meekness is an act of defiance. There's strength in it, though meekness isn't a condition that I wish to attain to receive a blessing. It's not about what you ought to do. It's just where you are.

James and I ended our conversation by talking about Jesus and the way he embodied meekness. How the Jesus brand of meekness is bold. How in the Beatitudes he is talking to people who have no choice but to be meek, the oppressed citizens of Judah under the power of Roman rule, and under those circumstances, Jesus talks and lives his way onto a cross.

James says:

That is spiritual rebellion, and this is the way that even I as a Jew can speak of Jesus dying for everyone. He literally talks his way onto a cross as a spiritual rebel, to be a sign for all of those people, and so I think you have to take him quite literally when he says, "I come not to bring peace but to bring strife." You can't ask people who are meek, who have been forced into meekness—you can't drag them up there with you . . . but you can show them there is a way to be a rebel from where they are.

• • •

I want to say again: This beatitude is not about striving to be anything. If we focus on meekness or humility as virtues to attain, we miss the point.

If I say I'm humble, what does that mean? It means I am not proud, right?

But what does the word mean? Where does it come from?

The word *humble* is related to the word *humiliate*—they have the same root.

So we could say that someone who is humbled is someone who has been humiliated. Some people say *humble* comes from the word *humus*, which literally means decomposed organic matter that is essential to the fertility of the earth. This announcement to the meek is for those who have been trodden into the ground. Those who are on the passive, receiving end of some humiliation.

Many teachers who are far cleverer and more scholarly than me have said that meekness means controlled strength. Some give the example of a wild horse that has been broken in and tamed. This beautiful beast still has wild strength, but its master can control it. But when I hear this explanation, all I can think is that once there was a beautiful wild animal, strong and free, and now it's not free at all. To me, an example of strength under control is Martin Luther King Jr., who gave his very life, his last bit of strength, seeking equality and justice for all. He remained strong and dignified in the face of racism and persecution and lived his message of peace and nonviolence until the end.

Being meek is not something we do. It's something we *are*— and often because it is forced upon us when we are oppressed, bullied, and marginalized, when the power of choice and opportunity and resources have been taken away, when our very presence is ignored and, if people see us at all, we are seen as the other and "less than."

And even in this, divine presence is offered and God invites us to carry on, to be strong and still open to what this life has to offer—because God is on our side.

HUNGER AND THIRST

Blessing or Requirement?

But I believe that the desire to
please you does in fact please you.

THOMAS MERTON

• • •

Blessed are those who hunger and thirst for
righteousness, for they will be filled.

MATTHEW 5:6

• • •

You're blessed when you've worked up a
good appetite for God. He's food and drink
in the best meal you'll ever eat.

MATTHEW 5:6, MSG

• • •

But under my skin is where you begin
And your kindness leads me now.

"OH MERCY (HUNGER AND THIRST),"
MATT MAHER, STU G, AND IAN CRON

A TIP: The next 275 words are best read with an English accent.

When we moved to America, one of the things we had to get used to was how folks greet each other. You'd think it would be the least of our worries. But it was confusing at times—so many choices! Once when I was picking up a rental car from an airport, I walked out to meet the guy who was going to give me my keys. Wanting to make a good impression, I'd narrowed my greeting down to two options:

- Howdy
- Hi

Really simple! Just pick one.

So I approached the man, a lovely older gentleman, and with my hand outstretched and my brain narrowing the choice further in my head, it all felt so easy. That is, until I opened my lips. I tripped over the words, and a glorious "*How*" came out of my mouth.

Embarrassing!

The one American greeting it took me a while to get the hang of was "Whassup." Now I'm not saying I don't know what it means—*What is up?* But I didn't know how to respond. I always wanted to answer with something like "Well, actually, I'm kinda feeling it today; we just moved over and everything's a bit unfamiliar and disorienting and we didn't know what dog food to get or laundry detergent" and so on. That's what's up!

What I didn't know was that the correct response would have been simply to say, "Whassup," back to the person. It's totally not required to enter into a dialogue about your well-being.

But I thought they cared.

I guess the equivalent I grew up with was:

Person 1: "All right, mate?"
Person 2: "Yeah, all right?"

So there we are. Is everything all right?

Well, probably not entirely. Not if we're like the people listening on the hill that day, the kind of people Jesus calls blessed.

Looking back at what we've seen so far: The Beatitudes are not about achieving anything, but about what's missing.

Our Teacher is announcing the incredible promise that here and now, in our poverty, sadness, and lack of power, when we can't get it right, God is on our side.

I like the way Frederick Bruner puts it: "God helps people who need help simply because they need help, not because they meet spiritual conditions."[1]

Jesus is also announcing that something's about to change, that a new way of looking at things is here, and more is coming. As N. T. Wright says, "[The Beatitudes are] an announcement, not a philosophical analysis of the world. It's about something that's starting to happen, not about a general truth of life. It is *gospel*: good news, not good advice."[2]

So there is something of a not-yet-ness to the Beatitudes. Jesus is announcing that the Kingdom of God is coming, and it's upside down from the way the world currently works. And it is really good news because God is with:

- the poor (and everyone whose spirit is crushed, the spiritual zeros, losers, those without a wisp of religion)
- those who mourn (the brokenhearted, the sad, the grieving)
- the meek (the powerless, the bullied, the average, the unnoticed, the overlooked)

These announcements are for those on the outside—the underneath, the undesirables, those for whom it really isn't working out. For whom everything is in fact *not* all right. And if you feel like this, if you're in that place, or if your heart is broken for people who are in that place—you're probably feeling hungry for a change.

And that's what this next beatitude is about—because inside that hunger is where the blessing is.

God is on your side.

•　•　•

Somewhere along the line somebody told me that I had to try really hard to do the right things, and that if I succeeded in doing the right things, then I'd really make it, I'd be someone, I'd be a success, I'd be blessed.

I used to think that being hungry and thirsty for righteousness was about striving and straining and obeying the rules, being morally pure and upright, without any guilt or shame. I used to think that what Jesus was saying was that if I try really hard to do this set of things, I can be like him—and then I'll be blessed.

But woe is me if I fail. Because the ones who make it in the end, the ones who get to be satisfied, are the ones who get it all right—and the ones who don't? Well, they won't!

And I don't get it all right . . . not all the time.

Because I'm an ordinary human being.

And oftentimes life is really hard and not good news.

Our Teacher announces that God is with us in the things that are absent, and not in the achievement of a set of spiritual virtues, so maybe to hunger and thirst for righteousness is not so much about trying to be super holy—but about living in the famine and desperation for God's righteousness and justice.

DESIRE

I'm a dreamer and I live in my head a lot, so I find myself longing for things often. I started to make a list the other day of some things I desire:

- I desire to do some good in the world.

- I've been married over thirty years and still really want to be a better husband. And not only that, but a better dad and a good son and an amazing grandpa (Pops).

- I desire that my daughters (and their families) find happiness and fulfillment, that they follow their dreams and become all that their incredible potential points to.

- I want to do good work. I hope this book and the music that I'm creating right now are the best work I've ever done. I really desire that.

- I've made mistakes along the way and have not always been the best version of myself. I want to learn from these things and make some changes.

- I desire to be a better guitar player, a better writer and songwriter.

- I'd really love to be in an amazing band again.

- I'd love to work more in India. I love that country! It has a pull on me.

- I truly desire to eat as much Indian food as I want—or Thai or barbeque or hot chicken—without piling on the pounds.

Okay, so I joke a bit. Sure, these are things that I desire. But all these desires pale in comparison to the thing that I desire above all else:

If God is real and there's this incredible force of renewal, love, and mercy in the universe, and if Jesus has shown us the way and invites us to a different way to live and be in the world, then I long for more of that reality. I desire to walk that way. I really do desire God more than anything else.

Thomas Merton, the Trappist monk from the Abbey of Gethsemani in Kentucky, wrote this prayer: "But I believe that the desire to please you does in fact please you. And I hope I have that desire in all that I am doing. I hope that I will never do anything apart from that desire. And I know that if I do this you will lead me by the right road, though I may know nothing about it."[3]

"The desire to please you."

That's what I'm talking about.

It's what Pope Francis calls the crack in the door[4]—the thing that lets the light of forgiveness and mercy in. It's the desire to take the step and not the step itself.

It's the hunger and thirst.

The absence, not the achievement.

The longing, not the action.

The desire, not the doing.

On the hill, Jesus speaks to this desire, despair, ache, longing, hunger, and thirst and says, "I am with you even in that!"

I have a hunch, though, that if this is my true desire, the other things will get taken care of (except, well, maybe that bit about eating whatever I want).

A little later in these words from the hill, we will hear our Teacher say, "Seek first his kingdom and his righteousness, and all these things will be given to you as well" (Matthew 6:33).

So the context there is Jesus urging his followers not to worry and get distracted about food and clothes and all the things we need to survive. He tells us to chill out and to seek the Kingdom of God and his righteousness.

And there's that word again: *righteousness*.

WHAT IS RIGHTEOUSNESS?

I have many friends who read *righteousness* as "justice," and I'm inclined to agree with them. When you see injustice in action, it's hard not to simply react with an ache and burning desire to see it put right. Like when I was in India and I met kids whose mothers were sex workers, and the kids had to hide under the bed or in a closet while their mums entertained clients—it just feels so wrong and you want it to be put right, don't you?

So *righteousness* does mean "justice." But remember, there are layers. These words have permanent surplus meaning. There's always more.

When we think about righteousness, we also get a sense of "I just want to live right"—you know, be a good person. Not in the self-righteous sense of the word, like "I'm better than you," but rather that you just want to be a good human and live well in the world. You want the internal struggles to be put right *and* the relationships around you to be good.

So that is what righteousness means as well: decency and harmony.

I asked my friend Brad Nelson, because he's smart, what righteousness looks like in the Bible. He told me that *righteousness* comes from the Greek word *dikaiosynē*, which essentially means, as Dallas Willard puts it, "true inner goodness." And then Brad told me that in the Hebrew Scriptures, *sedaqah* (Hebrew for "righteousness") is often found with *mispat* ("justice"). They are linked in the narrative arc of the Bible.

When Jesus' early listeners heard his words about hungering and thirsting for righteousness, they would have understood that Jesus meant doing the right thing regardless of the circumstances, and having a disposition toward justice no matter the cost.

Jesus the Jew was speaking out of a long Jewish tradition that God's desire for the world is *shalom*—peace, harmony, wholeness, completeness, everything in its right place (as Radiohead would say[5]). Nothing broken, nothing missing, proper relationships between us and God, us and each other, and us and the earth.

So maybe righteousness is all these things: a deep desire for *shalom* in our world.

Looking around on that hill, the mishmash of people knew very well what Jesus was talking about. Their world was broken, and they were being crushed. The Roman superpower had conquered, the fabric of their culture and the way things had been working for years was unraveling, and they were stuck paying high taxes and losing their inheritances and often becoming tenants on land that used to belong to them. The Roman occupation had radically changed the way the economy worked, and many people were literally hungry and thirsty, physically hurting for things to be different. They ached for everything to be put back together in its right place.

When we think about the world today, that starts to sound a little familiar, doesn't it?

So in the God story, which is still being written, the desperate longing for a personal righteousness comes hand in hand with the ache for things to be made right and for social justice for others. It's always been that way. Look at this:

> GOD, your God, is the God of all gods, he's the Master of all masters, a God immense and powerful and awesome. He doesn't play favorites, takes no bribes, makes sure orphans and widows are treated fairly, takes loving care of foreigners by seeing that they get food and clothing.
>
> You must treat foreigners with the same loving care—
>   remember, you were once foreigners in Egypt.
> DEUTERONOMY 10:17-19, MSG

In the Hebrew Scriptures, God's people are constantly reminded to look out for the orphan, the widow, and the stranger. When they forget this, forget to tell the story, a prophet such as Amos comes along and shows them the error of their ways.

So righteousness is this kind of complete goodness that is always bent towards justice. The divine gifts and grace of the Beatitudes will always have a social dimension and a requirement to see things put right.

And when wholeness and goodness and justice are missing, when we desire those things so much it hurts—in the ache, the longing, the craving, Jesus is saying, "You are blessed. God is on your side."

WHAT DO YOU ACHE FOR?

Have you ever wanted something so bad it hurt?

It's interesting that Jesus uses the words *hunger* and *thirst* to describe this—real physical feelings.

Several years ago back in the UK, we lived in a house not far from a pub, maybe a hundred yards or so down on the opposite side of the road, called the Smuggler's Roost. By the name you'd think it was built in the 1500s and might hold all kinds of secret nooks and crannies, but it was actually built in the 1960s and is now a Chinese restaurant.

Anyway.

It was quite fun, really. Friday and Saturday nights we'd lie in bed and hear groups of people making their way home, sometimes laughing or singing, sometimes fighting. We always hoped that our front fence would survive the late-night high jinks.

One night I was taking our dog for a walk, making my way down toward the beach, looking forward to the fresh salty air. Across the road, a man and woman were talking. They were having some sort of argument, but I didn't notice that at first.

I got about even with them when they suddenly erupted into shouting, and then the guy just started laying into the woman. Punching and kicking her. I couldn't believe it.

In that moment I was kind of stunned and shouted, "Hey!" Before I could even cross the road, the woman broke free and ran into the pub. At least she'd be safe in there.

I'm really glad she ran into the pub.

I hate confrontation, and I've never been in a fistfight. I probably would have got my nose broken, but I hadn't thought any of that through. I was just going to try to stand between them. I hate violence of any kind, but violence or abuse against women? I'm willing to suffer for that.

The point is not that I was a hero and took a few punches for a helpless maiden in distress—that would be a much better story. The point is, it left me with a guttural, actual ache. I wished their story were different, that it hadn't come to blows. And it brought to mind the wider issue of violent and abusive relationships. All of it left me feeling, *I just wish this was different.*

It's like you are *inside* the ache and the hurt.

And you can't fix it.

You just want it to change.

You want the wrongs made right.

I think a lot of us feel this ache for change. The world, and even our neighborhoods, are filled with the things that make us ache. Violence, poverty, racism, hunger, hatred, all kinds of injustice and loss.

Have you ever sat with the ache? Been familiar with that place?

Have you ever thought that the discomfort you feel is in fact being hungry and thirsty for righteousness and justice?

So what do you ache for?

Global Brokenness

We see it in our news feeds every day, but the shock never leaves. I am horrified at the displacement of people because of war and violence on the planet right now. In 2015, 65.3 million people were refugees, asylum seekers, or internally displaced, the most since World War II.⁶ That's one in every 113 people on the planet, more people than the population of France.

That's a lot of numbers, but when you remember that every number is a man, woman, or child with a name and family and pets and favorite toys . . . well, it just hurts.

And I ache for change.

I just watched a news clip of a family from Damascus reuniting in Germany. One member of the family had already made the trip. He got separated from his wife, sister, mother, and father and didn't know if they were going to survive the journey. But they did. It's happy because they were reunited, and sad because they just want to go home to Syria. But they can't, and as refugees they find themselves in a world split in terms of whether it wants to help them. Will they be welcomed or not wanted? As I write, as many as two thousand Syrian refugees arrive in Germany every day. And they are just the ones who make it!

This is a global problem. Millions of displaced people who just want to go home but can't are seeking refuge, and not many borders are friendly ones.

I recently talked to Jared Noetzel, who handles faith outreach for the ONE Campaign, an advocacy organization cofounded by Bono from U2 that works to end extreme poverty and preventable disease, especially in Africa. Their seven-million-plus members regularly take action, calling their leaders to end extreme poverty. They're passionate about providing equal opportunity for girls and women as well as helping refugees find hope and a future. I asked Jared what he aches for on a global scale, and his answer was fascinating.

Jared helped me see that most people, including myself, want to see policies and action. To ultimately see change for good as a result of that action. We want to see the wrongs made right. We want to see justice.

Jared explained that there's something to be said about the importance of political leaders here and that *advocacy* is a really key term in the conversation, since it denotes that we're focused on moving *leaders* to enact justice.

So that's what Jared aches for—advocacy, which is really the work of creating the space, the conversation, or the opportunity for justice to come about by the right actions of policymakers and political leaders.

From a scriptural standpoint, Esther and Mordecai are excellent examples of advocacy creating the opportunity for a secular, political ruler to do the right thing (that being the prevention of genocide). David even laid out what a political ruler who honors God should look like in Psalm 72 as a prayer for his son.

Jared went on to tell me:

Policy isn't everything, but it's a part that we can't overlook.
A lot of us understand the importance of caring for the
needs of the vulnerable. But advocacy is, and should be,
paired with direct service. That is, we as Christians should
both *do* what is righteous and just as well as *call* for
righteousness and justice in the laws that govern our land.

What I ache for is that this generation of Christians
would understand that their faith compels them to call
for justice through advocacy in a manner that's consistent
with Christ's example of loving neighbor and enemy.
We've a bit too easily forgotten that, sometimes because
we're more focused on success than faithfulness. We hope

and pray that the outcome of our persistent, hopeful advocacy will be justice, but we ought to acknowledge that we're not the source of justice.

Our job is to be faithful in doing what we're called to, specifically, to "speak up for those who cannot speak for themselves, for the rights of all who are destitute. Speak up and judge fairly; defend the rights of the poor and needy" (Proverbs 31:8-9).[7]

And I join him in that ache for change.

Communal Brokenness

Sometimes the ache is more local.

A few years ago I helped with a project called Awaken, out of the Dallas area. Some friends of mine were really engaged with low-income communities, and I had the bright idea of inviting some of the kids from the community to come and sing on a song or two for the album we were making.

I showed up for a couple of days, and we loaded our recording gear into a community room in the projects. Honestly, I felt like I did when I visited the Soweto township in South Africa. Here, I couldn't believe my eyes—dozens of kids noisily pushing past one another, excited to see this crazy Englishman. Then my friends told me the sort of work they do. If they didn't help the schools provide shoes for the kids, the kids would just have hand-me-down shoes that are falling apart at the seams. But the thing that really got to me was that if the schools didn't send these kids home with food at the weekend, the kids would go hungry and lack the nutrition needed to develop and even stay attentive to learning.

I wasn't expecting to see such poverty here. I couldn't believe this was America in the twenty-first century.

When I got home to Franklin in Williamson County, Tennessee, I started to dig around and found that the same was true here, in one of the wealthiest counties in America.[8] Just two miles from where I live, there are families on such low incomes that they rely on food pantries from organizations like One Gen Away, Graceworks, and Second Harvest. And in Williamson County alone, five thousand students qualify for free or reduced meal programs through the school systems.

And I ache for change.

Karen and I are a part of a church community in Franklin called Church of the City. Our pastor at COTC is Darren Whitehead, a fellow immigrant (except he's from Australia). Many years ago as a youth pastor, Darren was instrumental in bringing Delirious? to Franklin for a big event here in town. A few years after that, while he was working at Willow Creek Community Church in the Chicago suburbs, he brought us in to Willow for a couple of gigs. We have a history and friendship that I'm grateful for, and now he is back in Franklin as our pastor.

I spent some time with Darren to ask him what he aches for as a local church pastor in our city. He said,

When we started the church three years ago, we started two churches on the same day. One was in a poor community, and one was in a wealthy community.

And part of the reason we did that is that it's not just the poor who need the wealthy. The wealthy need the poor. Not only is Williamson County wealthy, but it's a religious community. I find that there is a spiritual hangover happening here right now—people are overchurched and underwhelmed, and I think that the opportunity that breaks the spell of this religious disillusionment is the wealthy serving the poor.

We come alive when we start to give sacrificially. Galatians says, "Bear one another's burdens,"[9] but you can't bear someone's burden if some of the burden is not actually falling on you. If you give out of excess, you're not actually sharing the burden. I think the challenge for us is that we need to give and we need to serve until some of the burden is falling on us.

Our church in East Nashville is walking distance from government-assisted housing, where people's average household income is $7,000 a year. And in Franklin, the average household income is $105,000 a year—almost a $2,000-per-week difference. And wealth and affluence is just as dangerous as poverty.[10]

Darren experienced a watershed moment in 2004 when he was a teaching pastor at Willow Creek and got to spend some time with Dr. John Perkins, who says, "The work of Justice is fundamentally redemptive. We are redeemed by God and then are invited to join the redemptive work of God."[11] Darren, like myself, didn't grow up here in the States and so didn't know the history of America and the civil rights movement. While Darren was in Chicago, someone had the idea to get twenty-five leaders from Willow—a large, predominantly white church—and twenty-five leaders from Salem Baptist—a large, predominantly African American church—and put them all on a bus for ten days to retrace the life, steps, and work of Dr. Martin Luther

King Jr. It was life changing, not only because of the cerebral experience of visiting the historic locations of the civil rights movement, but because Darren started building relationships with his African American brothers and sisters. This journey became a relational and emotional experience for all of them.

Dr. Perkins was leading this strange pilgrimage, and under his guidance Darren experienced the biblical text coming alive in a profound way. Learning, as I did, that righteousness and justice always show up together in Scripture changed everything for Darren.

So I straight up asked him: How does this work out in our life as a local church?

Well, we learned to our surprise that there are thousands of children in our county who are on government-assisted free or reduced-cost food programs through their schools. When schools let out for summer break, the children don't have access to those programs anymore, and they run the risk of not having enough food in their homes. So right there is a very specific challenge to the church: to be providing food so that these kids can have enough food while school's out. We partner with organizations like One Gen Away to help fill that gap.

Then there's foster care and adoption. We learned that there were three hundred children in Tennessee legally free to be adopted right now. Many of them have special needs or are older kids—and the urgency is that some of these kids will age out of the adoption program. They are going to become adults never having a family or belonging to a group of people.

Tennessee is a foster-to-adopt state—you have to foster first before you adopt. And we learned that there were only twenty-three families in all of Williamson County who were trained to do foster care. So think about it: the number of Christians, the number of churches, the number of God's people there must be in Williamson County . . . and there are so few homes for when a child needs to go to a foster home, they are sometimes putting them two hours away from where they know. So these kids can't go to the schools that they were in anymore—they just get pulled from their community. So, you know, this is a huge opportunity for the church to advocate for those who don't have a voice. These three hundred kids don't have a voice.

I know my own lack of engagement is often because I just don't see or know of the problems. Darren started to talk about the adoption crisis at church meetings and invited interested families to find out more about training to foster or adopt: "In our first meeting of people wanting to learn more, we had three hundred people show up! Remember, there are only twenty-three homes in the whole of Williamson County trained to take children currently. Now, already fifty people have started the training, so this initiative alone will triple the actual number of foster homes available here."

Darren reached out to the city to find out what problems the poor are facing and where the city needs help. Three things came back:

- reliable transportation
- housing
- affordable child care

Darren told me,

We've been able to significantly engage in two of these things. We are in the process of converting our child care school so that for every full fee-paying person, a subsidized person who wouldn't normally be able to afford it now can.

We also learned that single moms especially are like the widows in our society. What I mean by that is historically, the church is called to take care of orphans and widows, and I think single moms are like the modern-day widow. So much is against them—they are trying to be good moms, they're trying to raise their kids, yet they also have to work and provide. It's exhausting when you are living paycheck to paycheck.

What we learned is that when someone doesn't have the resources to get their vehicle fixed, then their life starts spiraling out of control. They aren't able to take their kids to school or to child care. They aren't able to get to their job. And they don't have the money to be able to get their car fixed.

So what we thought is that if the church can help them with car repairs or help them by giving them a reliable car, it's not so much a handout as a hand up. It's not so much an act of compassion as an act of justice. You're actually helping people help themselves.

Something as pragmatic as a car has such a disproportionate impact on these people's lives. They are able to thrive for themselves when they have a car. So what does the Acts 2 church look like in the twenty-first century? I think it looks like repairing people's cars for them.

At the time of writing, our church has plans to build auto repair bays on the church property. I love it! And it doesn't stop there. Darren said, "We are challenging the church that instead of trading your car in and upgrading it, give your car to the church, we'll give you a tax receipt for it, and then we'll give that car to people in need. Already we've given ten cars away, and we had another four given to us on Sunday. It's a game changer for these families."

There are a lot of us who go to church and have a lot more resources than many people do. We say we follow Jesus, but we're quite numb and sad and we don't have peace. I think what we've done is tried to combine the American dream with Christianity. I'm not sure those two things mix well. We need to be set free from that. And maybe the way we get set free is to hunger and thirst for righteousness and justice, and to let the ache disrupt us into action until we become part of the solution.

When we ache for change, all we need to do is see what God is doing in our communities.

Personal Brokenness

Something eats you up. You made a huge mistake in a relationship and wish you could make it right, but the damage is done. You wonder if it can ever be put right.

You watch as your friends' marriage falls apart in slow motion before your eyes, and there's so much hurt and devastation. You want it to get fixed so bad it literally messes with your insides.

And you ache for change.

There's this tension because you just went on a trip and learned about the dire circumstances of extreme poverty in a foreign land. You know that once you have seen, you can't un-see. But you're going home to upgrade your home, and at the same time there's some kind of responsibility. There's a wrestling match going on inside your soul, and you don't know how to live with the tension.

And you ache for change.

Sometimes it's an intense personal desire for change inside yourself. The ache when you wake up in the morning and can't believe you did that thing again last night. That thing that seems to have a power over you that you can't break. That itch that builds up and builds up, and then in a moment of unconditional surrender you scratch just to get some relief. That addiction, that secret, that thing that numbs reality—and you just wish it were different, but you can't beat it. It's in control.

You failed again.

You can't fix it.

It goes too deep.

And you ache for change.

And it's in *that* desire, *that* longing, *that* ache, *that* hunger, *that* thirst—in the absence of righteousness and justice, not the achievement of it—that Jesus announces you're blessed. God is with you. God is on your side.

GETHSEMANE

I just got back from the Holy Land, where I was struck again by the power of the story of Gethsemane. Walking in that garden of ancient olive trees, sitting in the silent meditation of the Church of All Nations overlooking Jerusalem, it's hard to imagine the ache, anguish, and agony of a prayer that makes you sweat blood: "My Father, if there is any way, get me out of this. But please, not what I want. You, what do *you* want?" (Matthew 26:39, MSG).

And I think about the things I long for and the choices I have to make. Sometimes being alive to the path of righteousness and justice seems impossibly hard. It hurts.

Being hungry and thirsty—indeed, the very ache itself for global, communal, and personal change—is a sign that we actually understand. A sign that we *get it*.

And there on the hill, Jesus speaks to this desire, despair, ache, longing, hunger, and thirst and says: *I am with you even in that.*

5

MERCY

Getting Caught in the Rain

God's mercy can make even the driest land become
a garden, can restore life to dry bones.

POPE FRANCIS, EASTER 2013

• • •

Blessed are the merciful,
for they will be shown mercy.

MATTHEW 5:7

• • •

You're blessed when you care.
At the moment of being 'care-full,'
you find yourselves cared for.

MATTHEW 5:7, MSG

• • •

Close your eyes and lay down your head
Looks like you could use some rest
That's what Mercy says
And when you wake up
You're gonna shine with the morning light—again

"MORNING LIGHT," AMY GRANT AND STU G

IT WAS 3:00 A.M., and she was walking down the double yellow line in the middle of the road. Most of the girls walked the sidewalks, but not Dorris. Walking the middle of the street may have seemed brash and confident, but Dorris was on that yellow line because she was afraid of the dark. The shadows of the doorways and alleys held memories that no one should have to think about.

And every night of the twenty years she had walked the yellow line, she recited the Twenty-third Psalm: "Even though I walk through the valley of the shadow of death, I will fear no evil" (ESV).

It hadn't always been this way.

There had been happier times, a long time ago. When she was a child, her dad would put her on his knee and sing with her. Dorris loved to sing. He would carry her to church and take her up to the front to sing with the choir. She held on to those misty memories as she walked the yellow line.

She missed her dad.

When Dorris was twelve years old, a deranged family member walked into their home and shot her mother and father. Her mum was seriously injured. Her dad was killed. Dorris ran to him as he was shot and was trapped under his falling body.

Can you imagine the horrific trauma? At twelve years old, Dorris discovered that marijuana numbed her pain. She became addicted to being numb. As adulthood arrived, so did cocaine, and the ensuing twenty-year addiction led her to the streets of Nashville. And to the yellow line.

To get the next fix, to escape the heat or the cold, to get the next meal—whatever the reason—she would get into any car that stopped for her. More than once she'd been found in a ditch, left for dead after getting into the wrong car with the wrong person. She had seen so many men and women die on the streets, and maybe this was her lot too. Maybe this was the last time she would walk the yellow line.

In and out of cars, in and out of seedy rooms, in and out of jail—this was her life, and what kind of life was it? Surely she had messed up so completely that there was no hope.

But even while she was high, even as she walked the yellow line, she could still hear herself say the words "The LORD is my shepherd; I shall not want" (Psalm 23:1, ESV).

Then one day, during one of her stints in jail, Dorris saw a familiar face, a friend she had walked and worked the streets with. Dorris had not seen Regina Mullins for ten years. She had just assumed that Regina was dead—but there she was, radiant and alive. Regina was not an inmate, but a visitor talking to a group of inmates, addicts, and prostitutes about something called Magdalene House.

Regina saw Dorris, and her eyes lit up. "Dorris, guess what?" she said. "I got my life back!"

Dorris was skeptical. "How did you do that?" she asked.

"I found this place called Magdalene," Regina told her. "Come on—come over!"

Dorris shook her head. "I can't. I've tried so many times to get clean. I go to halfway houses and then I find a little job, but as soon as the money gets in my hand my addiction kicks back in. I spend my rent, then I have to go sleep with somebody to pay the rent, and then I feel guilty about using, and I go on using because I feel guilty. I can't stop it. I can't do it."

Regina nodded. She understood the cycle Dorris felt trapped in. "Dorris, just don't worry about it. This place is totally different from any place I've ever known. And we don't ask you to pay the rent."

Regina gave Dorris the number for Magdalene House and told her to call when she was getting out. Told her to hold on, told her to hang on in there—Regina would be in touch.

Last week, I got to sit down and talk with a survivor of rape and abuse. Of prostitution, of trafficking and drug addiction. Her name is Dorris.

She made the call.

She went to Magdalene.

She got her life back.

She has a job at Thistle Farms in Nashville.

She still sings *all* the time. In fact, Dorris leads the choir at her church.

And that, my friends, is what mercy does.

• • •

As I read the Beatitudes, I wonder if this announcement of mercy right in the middle here is actually the punch line. Maybe the invitation to show mercy and to receive it is the key to what life is all about.

Mercy broods over and permeates the first four announcements, the ones to people who haven't chosen their situations. These first four announcements are what Frederick Dale Bruner calls the "need" or "poor" beatitudes—the surprising God-bless-yous to those in awful situations.[1]

The promise of presence in your poverty:

when your spirit is crushed,

when you are brokenhearted,

when you are overpowered and pushed to the side,

when you ache for wholeness and justice.

And in the midst of these things, what we find here is presence. An invitation to carry on, with God on our side. We receive mercy in the depths and darkness of our greatest needs.

And mercy carries on into the next three beatitudes, the ones Bruner calls the "help" beatitudes.[2] These beatitudes are a kind of "doing" or "service," but it's not doing or serving to attain any kind of blessing or recognition. Rather this is about *being*: It's what we *become* by accepting the invitation to join God in the work he's already doing, and being where he is. By showing mercy.

Around and around it goes. We receive mercy. We show mercy. And we receive mercy when we are found to be showing mercy.

I love that Pope Francis announced 2016 as an extraordinary jubilee—the Holy Year of Mercy.[3] That he sees mercy as Jesus' most important message. Because God never tires of showing mercy.

Receiving mercy is like having a crushing weight lifted off your chest. It's like fresh air bursting into suffocating lungs.

But what *is* mercy, really?

When you search for a definition of *mercy* online, this is what comes up: "Compassion or forgiveness shown towards someone whom it is within one's power to punish or harm."[4]

That's cool, but let's be honest—it's not how we live, is it? *Mercy* is not a word we use every day unless we go to church a lot, and then it kind of falls off the tongue—"Lord, have mercy" . . . "grace and mercy." Flattened and overfamiliar words to most of us. Outside the walls of the church, we don't hear the word *mercy* very much. And we don't see a whole lot of it lived out. Our world is one that often seems to be stripped of mercy.

I thought about mercy when I saw the shocking images of twenty-one Coptic Christians dressed in orange, paraded on a beach, about to have their heads cut off. If I'd been among their number that day, I would have been begging for mercy. And I did actually beg for mercy, in a knee-jerk reaction: "Lord, have mercy on us, this human race, that we have the capacity to behave like this."

A PLACE OF MERCY

I called Rabbi Joseph and explained to him that I had a gut feeling, a hunch, for this book and the music I'd be creating around the idea of mercy—that the mercy chapter should be stories of women, and the song should be a woman's voice. He didn't hesitate: "You are absolutely right," he said. "The root of the Hebrew word from which we get mercy means *womb*. Mercy comes from the womb of God."[5]

Stunning.

My friend and counselor Al Andrews had told me often about the work of Thistle Farms, a place of mercy sung over and over in the voices of hundreds of women. He invited me to go take a visit with him. So I did, and I wasn't quite ready for what I was about to experience.

Thistle Farms is a beautiful nonprofit work started by Rev. Becca Stevens, an Episcopal priest in Nashville. It's a powerful community of women who have survived prostitution, trafficking, and addiction. Thistle Farms employs more than fifty survivors through their social enterprises, which include a natural body care company, Thistle Stop Café, an artisan studio, and a global marketplace called Shared Trade. Thistle Farms also includes Magdalene House, a two-year residential program with advocacy services for up to seven hundred women yearly, and stands for the truth that, in the end, love is the most powerful force for change in the world. I'm in awe of their work. (Search for the hashtag #LoveHeals and you'll see what I mean.)

I got to chat with Becca, and because she's a busy lady, I had a few questions written down so as to not waste any of her time. She disarmed me straightaway with her genuine Southern charm, told me we had loads of time, and wanted to talk about the Beatitudes. She told me,

> The Beatitudes have been the core of how I've lived and worked forever. My first memory is my dad's death when I was five. He was a priest, and the Gospel at his funeral was the Beatitudes, and at my wedding the Gospel was the Beatitudes, and at my children's baptisms the Gospel was the Beatitudes. Whole communities have been founded around the Beatitudes.
>
> If you are trying to get to a place where you love without judgment and you welcome everybody and leave nobody behind, you have to work from the Beatitudes. They are the heart of the gospel. It's how we live.[6]

Becca has been a priest since the early nineties, and for most of that time, she has been working with and loving on women who have been sexually abused, addicted, or on the street. When I asked her how her own story inspired her work of mercy, she said,

> After my father died, the guy that came in to run the church sexually abused me for a couple of years. I would

say that what happened to me sowed the seeds of awareness and compassion for women who are walking the streets.

You know, the lines that people think separate us—you're an artist, I'm a priest, Regina is a recovering prostitute—those lines mean nothing. We all have experiences of brokenness *and* mercy, and I think, what I've known in my life, is that our stories aren't finished. Our stories are not just our past—our stories are also our hopes and dreams. My biggest longing is that each story is one of healing and each story is one of hope. If you have that desire, then you have to be in community with people.

There is no life without brokenness, and mercy is always there. So I don't put people's brokenness on a scale, and I don't put people's experience of mercy on a scale either. We all have this longing: to be loved and to love. To have meaning in our lives and to be part of something bigger than ourselves.

When you walk into Thistle Farms, the atmosphere is tangible. It's like the whole building is thick with transformation, with renewal, with healing—with mercy.

And at Thistle Farms, I got to meet Regina Mullins for myself. Becca says that Regina is just as much a founder of the work as she is.

Regina is the residential manager of Magdalene House at Thistle Farms. She showed me around one of the homes, which houses seven women in recovery. It was incredible. But what was just as incredible was her own story. She had been on the streets in Nashville, caught up in a life of drugs and prostitution from '81 to '97, and had been to jail so many times. One night when Regina was on the street, crack pipe in hand, she looked up at the sky and said, "God, if you're real, you see what I'm going through, do something! I don't wanna die out here."[7] She wanted out. And the only place of safety, where she would not have to turn any tricks, was in jail. So when some cops drove by and told her to get off the streets, she refused. When they drove by a second time, she picked up a rock and threw it at the car—and the police had no option but to arrest her. She was granted her wish of a jail cell for the night. However, because of previous trouble, one night turned into two and a half years. She eventually made parole but was scared of falling back into her old life.

While still in prison, she received a call from a friend who used to be incarcerated with her, and her friend told her about this priest who had started a household to help women like them start a new life. There were four girls in the house and five beds. Would she like the last space?

At first Regina was really skeptical. Life had taught her that nothing was free. But with going back on the streets the only other option, she decided to go to the house.

What she found was a beautiful home with real beds and furniture and a nice kitchen with pots and pans—and help, friendship, health care, trust, and a new life. And it was all paid for.

It looked and felt a lot like mercy.

When Regina arrived at the house, she was expecting to see a priest in a black shirt with a white collar and was really worried because she thought, *If I need to go to confession every day, it's gonna take years, cuz honey . . . I got a lot of confessin' to do.*

Then her friend introduced her to Becca. Regina says, "I saw this blonde girl who looked just like us, in Daisy Duke shorts and a baby on her hip." Strangest-looking priest Regina ever saw.

Becca told Regina to just come and live and relax. This was sanctuary, and Becca wanted her to decide what she wanted for her life, and whatever Regina would decide positively, Becca was going to walk with her. This was her way out.

That's what Becca did, and that's what Becca and her team continue to do, and that's what Regina does for the women who have come behind her.

Regina's vision, with Thistle Farms and Magdalene House, is to show women love. To tell them that they are loved, they are worthy, and they are not the scum of the earth, no matter what others may tell them. That they can get husbands and get their families back and they can be good mothers and they can work legal jobs and survive.

Regina showed me some candles. "We light one of these for each of our friends and loved ones who are still out there. We light them so they can find their way home."

●　●　●

Mercy has helped Jennifer find her way home.

Born in Dayton, Ohio, and raised Catholic, Jennifer had a mother whose love was nonexistent and an abusive, alcoholic father who suffered from PTSD. She also had an uncle who would sexually assault her often. While she does have some good childhood memories, they are largely clouded out by the bad ones. So when at twelve years old she was offered weed, she discovered it helped her cope with the pain and also gave her courage to stand up to her abusers. It felt like freedom. She became defiant and unruly—and ran away from home.

"When you're a young, lost, runaway child," she told me, "you immediately become a target for pedophiles, human trafficking, child pornographers, and that's basically what happened to me."[8]

Jennifer was thirteen years old when she climbed into a truck at a truck stop for the first time.

> I told the truck driver, "I'm gonna go out to LA and become a movie star. I don't need home anymore." Because of the abuse, I really was an addicted, defiant woman trapped in a child's body. But I still had hopes and dreams. He knew exactly what to say: "Oh, I'm going all the way out there, I'm gonna take care of you, I'm gonna buy you new things." And I'm like, *Oh yay, this is it!* But when he pulled into the next truck stop, I knew what was going to happen. He put me in the back of the bed and climbed in behind me. It all happened really fast. After, he threw some money back in there and said, "Get dressed." He called out on his CB and said, "I have a sweet young thing here. She'll take care of you if you take care of her." And he got an immediate response. When he was taking me to my next ride, I wasn't really shocked by what just had happened 'cause I'd experienced this before. It was that he lied to me—that was the shock. He said he was gonna take care of me, he said he was gonna do this, and I really did believe him, you know.

Jennifer was passed from truck to truck up and down the East Coast and as far west as Joplin for four years. There was a huge trafficking ring hidden in the secret depths of the trucking world.[9]

At sixteen she met a man and fell in love. Found out she was pregnant, turned seventeen, and married the guy all in four months. She had her first son, James, and he became everything she lived for. Her husband was messing around, but James brought joy to Jennifer's life for the first time that she could remember. At nineteen she became pregnant again, but this time there were complications and she had to be on bed rest for four months. When she went into labor, she thought, *We are going to make it*, but the baby's heart stopped moments before he was delivered. There was nothing that could be done. Jennifer says,

It was like a light switch going off. Everything went dark.

I dropped James off with my mother, I divorced my husband, and I started working in the sex industry. It made sense to me that I charged for it. When you're young and you look the part, it's reasonably acceptable in the world. There's a billion-dollar sex industry out there. But every time I sold myself—every time I put a drug in me—a piece of me died, and it evolved into over twenty years of homelessness, injecting heroin, in and out of jail, psych wards. I was insane. I never grieved my son. I never went to the funeral. I shut down completely. I hardened my heart. It was such a darkness, and I thought I was gonna die.

But Jennifer didn't die. She became pregnant again and had an abortion, which made her very ill. After that she had a baby girl, Marie, then another daughter, Lianna. Jennifer then had

twins—John and Joseph—and then another son, Benjamin.
John, Joseph, and Benjamin she gave up for adoption; all the
other children her mother raised. She said that her kids knew
her only as the lady who sent them Jolly Ranchers in letters
from jail.

As a young adult, Lianna went looking for Jennifer. She found
her when Jennifer asked her own daughter for directions to a
homeless shelter and didn't recognize her.

Reconnecting with her family after years showed Jennifer that
she needed help. And so she found her way to mercy and healing
at Thistle Farms. I asked Jennifer what mercy looks like to her,
and she had so much to say:

> Now God's mercy—oh my goodness, let me tell you
> first about when I arrived at Thistle Farms and got
> into Magdalene. I experienced unconditional love;
> I was treated with dignity when I hadn't been treated
> with dignity in so long. Love is the only thing that will
> soften hard hearts, and believe me, I had a hard heart.
>
> When I came to work here at Thistle Farms in
> September of 2010, they put me in the paper studio, and
> I'm like, really? This is what I'm doing, making paper? I'm
> taking all this old paper and garbage and stuff and mixing
> it together and turning it into paper. But in the end it
> became very healing for me: taking all the unwanted
> things and turning them into something valuable.
>
> I also had Hep C when I arrived here at Thistle Farms,
> contracted because of twenty years of heroin needles every
> day. The methadone clinics tried to get me to quit because
> they knew I had Hep C, but I didn't care—you know, I'm

on the streets and it's like, God, why am I not dead yet? My viral levels were so high when I got here that they sent me to Dr. Perry at Vanderbilt to treat my liver for Hep C. He says, "Jennifer, your viral levels are skyrocketing. We're gonna put you on these drugs—it's like chemo for your liver. It's gonna pull the rug out from underneath you, it's gonna knock you down, so it's a good thing you're in a long-term recovery house!" I say, "All right, let's do it. I came here to heal." This was right about the time I started at Thistle Farms. As it came up to Christmas, I'm talking to Dr. Perry and he says, "You know what, you've waited several years—a couple more months is not gonna matter. Wait until January, call me back, and we'll get you started on the treatment."

So I was making this thistle paper and went in in January 2011 so they could check my blood to make sure they gave me the right dose. After, Dr. Perry called me and said, "Jennifer, your viral levels are so low, we can't even give you treatment! Come back every three months so we can check!"

I know it was a miracle. We witness modern-day miracles here every day. It's resurrection—it's where the dead come to life—it's God's grace and mercy all around us. I have been back, and I still have not had treatment for my liver. I went back in 2015 and they still cannot detect it. I've been healed because I surrendered to mercy.

All the women I've met at Thistle Farms have received mercy: unconditional love, compassion, kindness, hope, freedom out of a life of brokenness. Each has been able to rebuild her life in order to offer mercy to other women seeking healing out of brokenness themselves.

Making friends at Thistle Farms has been a really beautiful part of this journey. The stories of mercy, renewal, and restoration are astonishing. But it's easy to see these women as victims. It's easy to think that it makes sense for them to receive mercy, to get a chance at new life. But what about offering mercy to the offender, the abuser, the violator?

•   •   •

I was stunned when I watched a YouTube video of a man named Ricky Jackson being released from the prison where he'd spent thirty-nine years for a murder crime he did not commit.[10] A twelve-year-old boy in 1975 testified against him under duress, and that piece of evidence put Ricky away. Thirty-nine years later the boy—now a man—went to court and retracted his testimony, saying he'd lied because he thought he was helping. Thought he was doing the right thing. When he was released, Ricky was asked what he thought of the man. Ricky forgave him. He said it took a lot of courage for this man to do what he did. He recognized that the guy had also carried that burden for thirty-nine years.

All that time in prison, innocent, falsely accused—and now free, with forgiveness on his lips—Ricky's face was a picture of joy and relief.

So Ricky's story got me thinking. I wondered if there was someone whose life had been filled with impossible choices, and whose behavior deserved punishment—but who had been shown mercy by the system, by the state, by the ones with the power to punish or harm. What would mercy look like, feel like, to someone who had been granted it in exuberant abundance? When it was not expected or deserved?

Al Andrews told me about his friend Gaile, a survivor of twenty-four years on death row. I was intrigued and asked if I could meet her. But just hearing about her gave me a crazy idea. I'd been wrestling with this Beatitudes Project, thinking about this book and songs we could craft around it. And we hadn't written a mercy song yet. What would the song look like if it pulled from a story like this?

I bumped into Amy Grant when I played a show with her and Michael W. Smith. When Amy asked me what was going on in my world, I told her that I'd been dreaming about creating a project based on the themes of the Beatitudes for years. Amy seemed really interested.

I plucked up courage and asked if she would consider writing a song with me, and she said yes. I was caught off guard because I wasn't expecting such a swift and enthusiastic response—but even then, it took me a few months before I plucked up the courage to call her with my idea.

"Amy—I've got this idea to listen to a story from a lady who spent twenty-four years on death row," I told her. "And to write a song and tell her story from the point of view of what mercy looks like to her." Amy agreed immediately, said, "I love to cook," and invited us all around for lunch.

It was a beautiful late August day when one by one we arrived at Amy's house. She had prepared a very tasty lunch, and after we said our hellos we sat down to eat and chat. And it was there that I listened to one of the most extraordinary stories I've ever heard.

In 1985, Gaile Owens was arrested and charged as accessory before the fact to her husband's murder. On January 15, 1986,

she was found guilty and sentenced to death by lethal injection.
When we talked that day at Amy's house, Gaile had been out of
prison on parole for three and a half years. That meant she had
been on death row for twenty-four years.

As she was sitting next to me—thirty years after that terrible
day in 1985—I could not imagine a sweeter, kinder person.
I knew there had to be layers upon layers of her story, so I simply
asked Gaile to share the bits of her story she felt comfortable with.
My overarching question was *What does mercy look like to you?*

Gaile immediately started talking about her life as a little
girl, and mainly it centered on her father. She had grown up in
a Pentecostal background, but her dad didn't go to their church.
Gaile's father's struggle with the church and its legalism meant he
didn't attend with the family. He did, however, own several service
stations and financially supported the church his wife and kids
were attending. For him it was about supporting the people.

"Daddy used to sing," Gaile said. "He had one of the most
beautiful baritone voices I ever heard. We used to sing together
at home." But, she told me, "Daddy was an alcoholic, and he
was just trying to mask the things that bothered him. That's
what started the downside of our family stories. He was an
'every-three-day drunk.'"[11]

One Christmas, after her son, Stephen, had been born, Gaile
invited the family to come to their house on Christmas Day.
When her dad arrived late because he was hung over, Gaile confronted him:

I said, "Why can't you stop drinking?"
He said, "You never wanted for anything!"
I said, "Yes I did! I wanted you!"

Gaile's father broke down in tears and didn't get drunk again . . . until Gaile was arrested. He died five years after she was incarcerated.

Then Gaile told us about visiting her uncle's farm as a little girl, and how from the age of seven years old she experienced sexual abuse there. "I loved the farm, and I would go visit and explore the sheds and the barn and see the animals and stuff, and there was so much of it that was beautiful," she said. "But I didn't know what to do with the abuse. It was hard, and then, when I grew up, I married an abusive man." She paused. "And I lived in that marriage for thirteen and a half years."

No one knew about the abuse. Gaile was desperate to hold the family together. There were few shelters for women to go to in the eighties, and there was no divorce in her family or her church, which was hyper-legalistic. Her boys were all she had, and she would do anything not to lose them.

She continued, "I used to think, *God, why can't you just fix it?* 'Cause I loved him [her husband, Ron]. I didn't love what he did, I didn't love that, but I didn't hate him. I have two beautiful sons because of him, and their journey has been difficult because they couldn't figure out how to love their dad's memory and love me, too."

After she was arrested, Gaile admitted everything. She took full responsibility for her actions, and when a plea bargain was offered, she signed it straightaway. It meant if she pleaded guilty, she would be given a life sentence and wouldn't have to testify and drag the family through a trial. *But*—and it's a *big* but—the other person involved in the crime had to agree to plead guilty and sign the plea bargain as well. That person refused.

The prosecutors withdrew the deal.

It meant that they had to go to trial, but Gaile refused to take the stand and give evidence, wanting to save her sons from the details and the pain of the life that had been hidden from them.

"I am so ashamed of what I did," she says. "I wish I could go back and change it, but I can't. I've accepted responsibility for putting the wheels in motion that led to Ron's death. I pled guilty to the crime so my family would not have to go through any more than they were already suffering. I did not want to say in court what had happened to me. Just give me the life sentence and leave my kids alone."

Gaile never took the stand in her defense. The jury never heard a word of the abuse she suffered as a wife or as a child. There was evidence of abuse, but none of this evidence was made available to the defense or the jury in the trial. So in January of 1986, Gaile was the first person in Tennessee legal history to agree to a life sentence but receive the death penalty instead. When her twelve-year-old son, Stephen, testified in court that day, it was the last time he and his mother would see each other for decades.

Stephen and Brian had lost their father and their mother all at once.

Gaile had to get used to life in prison, life on death row. The death sentence ever present and hanging over her. At first she was on lockdown twenty-three hours a day, allowed out of her eight-by-ten concrete cell for an hour—shackled—to shower, exercise, and make a phone call if she needed to. She had a lot of time to think.

On June 6, 1986, she woke up crying, and she didn't know why. It was just tears from the bottom of her gut. Her Pentecostal upbringing had taught her about the do's and don'ts and the consequences of failure. She didn't have a concept of a merciful Father who is never tired of forgiving.

She says,

It wasn't like something had happened and I was weeping over it. It was from every part of my being. I cried probably for eight hours that day. I couldn't eat. I couldn't do anything. Part of the day I'd be on the floor, part of the day I'd be on the bed, and it just would not stop. My body hurt so bad from just the riveting of my body from the tears, and I just believe that's where I just emptied my soul of everything and said, "God, just make me what you want me to be and I'll do that."

For comfort, Gaile would sing to herself her favorite song. Amy Grant's "My Father's Eyes."

She never thought in a million years she would be sitting at this table, telling Amy Grant and a bald Englishman her story.

Gaile made her peace with God that day and knew beyond any doubt that she was forgiven. She was reconciled to the situation. She would either live and one day be forgiven by her family, or she would be executed and be with God. The one thing she wanted was to not harm her sons any more than they had already been harmed.

Over time it became clear to the warden and the prison authorities that Gaile wasn't a danger to other prisoners, and they gradually allowed her to become part of the wider prison population. Her first "job" was doing paperwork in the property cage, where she worked alongside two other inmates. Interacting with other people felt good.

After six years of solitary confinement, she received a policy exemption, allowing her to be placed in the general population, in nonsegregated living. As the only inmate on death row, Gaile welcomed this gladly. And here, Gaile came into her own—as a friend, employee, teacher, role model, mentor, leader, and volunteer.

She was given a job doing clerical work. "It was the first time I ever saw a fax machine or a computer," she said. Gaile got another job working for TennCare inside the prison, and part of that job involved answering phone calls. She had not answered a phone in eight years.

She was elected by her fellow inmates to the Inmate Council, where she was a voice for her peers at monthly meetings. Gaile became someone that other inmates, especially the young, trusted and would talk to. "I could defuse most tense situations," she told us. "People just need to feel like someone is hearing them sometimes."

When Gaile was telling us her many stories of life in prison, one in particular stood out to me:

> I found something I could do there in the prison. Women come in all the time from the jails, and they don't have shower shoes—and they have to get in a communal shower without shoes, which is not good. I realized that we sold these shower shoes for seventy-nine cents a pair. I could only buy three pairs a time—that was the limit— so I started buying three pairs of shower shoes every week and putting them in a box in my office. When I got fifty pairs bought up, I went to the unit manager and I said, "I wanna tell you what the shower shoes are about."

I said, "Today, when those five new admissions come in, if anybody doesn't have shower shoes, I wanna give them a pair. And when they get their money, they can buy me a pair to put back in my box so that I can give it to the next person."

There were a few that never paid it back, but the word got out on the compound after about a year, and people said, "Why didn't Gaile tell us? We would give shower shoes to it." So they were hauling them from the annex, hauling them from anywhere, and there was this room that had nothing in it but shower shoes. So that way I got to interact with every new person.

Gaile then said thoughtfully,

I got to sit down with these young girls that came in, and they would say, "Ms. Gaile, I can't do this, it's two years, I can't do it." I'd say, "Let me tell you this: You lost the very same thing I did when I came to prison twenty-whatever years it was ago, so it's just as important to you. You've lost family; you've lost a support system. But you will make it, and if you do like you need to, you'll walk out better than you walked in."

That's how it was. Gaile offered mercy by helping orient new inmates to prison life—listening to them, guiding them, and giving them shower shoes.

There is not enough space in a single chapter to tell the whole of Gaile's story. Of all the people she helped, of all the struggles she had and still has, of all the people who got to know her and love her and who wanted to help and speak up for her and see her death sentence commuted to a life sentence. Of how she would pray every day to see her boys just one more time before she died so she could ask forgiveness.

That day came after she had been incarcerated for twenty-three years. Stephen Owens filled in the forms and went to see his mum. Gaile says:

> The warden came in and shook his hand when Stephen came to visit that day, and she said, "We've prayed for this for years." That doesn't happen in the prison system. So Stephen comes in, and of course we're both emotional as we can be and crying. And then I hugged my daughter-in-law and 'course, I knew her because they had been on the same T-ball team and bowling team as kids, and this is who he ended up marrying.
>
> We were only supposed to visit for an hour, but they let me visit for three hours. We talked about fun times that we remembered. He told me where people had moved and what people that I had known were doing and the church and all that stuff.
>
> We talked about school and talked about the babies, and then the prison guards came to see me: "Gaile, you have five minutes." I didn't even realize it was three hours, and he didn't either. And so I said, "Stephen, before you leave . . ."
>
> He said, "Mom, I don't know whether I'll be back or not . . . I just needed to make this visit." And he said, "You can call, we'll talk on the phone, but I just don't know if I can come back." And I told him I understood.

So I told him, "There's one thing I need to ask you. I just need you to forgive me. When you walk out of here, I need to know that you have."

And he looked at me and said, "That's what I'm here for. To tell you that you're forgiven."

And that's how our visit ends. Lisa [Stephen's wife] tells this story of him walking out the back down to the car, asking him, "Are you okay?" And he said, "I'm fine. If I'd known the weight on my shoulders would be as light as it is right now, I would have done this years ago. I didn't realize what I carried with it."

By law there is a process allowing seven appeals for clemency, and as the years rolled by, Gaile still didn't want to testify to the abuse and drag the family through more pain and dirt. Each appeal had failed. In 2009 there was only one more left. That last appeal to save Gaile's life was denied by the Tennessee Supreme Court. A date was set for her execution.

But Gaile's son was instrumental in helping a team of lawyers and friends publicly tell Gaile's story and start a petition campaigning for a commutation.[12] The last hope was an appeal to the governor of Tennessee, Phil Bredesen.

Governor Bredesen agreed to look at the facts and make a decision. However, no one knew when that would be or what the outcome would be. He promised the team he would not wait until the last minute.

On July 14, 2010, Gaile was called to the counselor's office.

I go in there thinking she wants a memo or something. She goes, "Gaile, you need to stand here. Your attorneys are fixing to call you." I said, "What?" She said, "Yep, the warden called and said for me to have you stand right here." So I answer the phone, and my attorneys said, "Bredesen's fixed to make an announcement. We're headed to the steps of the courthouse. We'll call you as soon as we know something." And my stomach just went! I turned around, and all the staff realize what the phone call's about. They're all crying, and I went, "What are you crying for?" They said, "We're just so excited and we're so nervous—and you're not crying." I said, "Will y'all stop! Please!"

So here comes the phone, it's ringing—well, you could have heard a pin drop! On the other end they had connected Stephen and my two attorneys, and Stephen is crying.

And he says, "Mom, we did it."

Tears
Relief
Joy
Mercy

Governor Bredesen commuted Gaile's death sentence to a life sentence, taking off a thousand days of sentence credit.

Bredesen cited two considerations. First, that there was at least a possibility she had been in an abusive marriage. It didn't excuse anything but should have been taken into consideration when sentencing. And second, that she was offered a plea bargain prior to the trial—life imprisonment for her guilty plea, which she accepted, along with the responsibility and the punishment.

In an extraordinary twist in her story, unusual for someone who was guilty and given the death sentence, Gaile made parole. The decision came on September 28, 2011. One year after the day Gaile Owens would have been executed.

On October 7, 2011, Gaile walked out of the Tennessee Prison for Women with a single box of possessions and the clothes she was wearing. Stephen and his wife, Lisa, were waiting for her along with a small group of friends so vital to her story.

I cannot imagine what it was like for Gaile to enter prison in 1985 and leave in 2011. The world has changed so much in that time! Cell phones, the Internet, and so much more.

Gaile also had to set about reestablishing her identity, open a bank account, get a driver's license and Social Security number, amongst many other things.

Gaile says,

I had one of the biggest support systems of anybody coming out of prison, but I'mma tell you right now, you can't have a support system big enough for the day-to-day things that get up in your face, and that you don't understand and you don't know what to do. I always thought I was pretty quick on my feet—not the brightest star in the universe, but I wasn't dumb by any means of the imagination. First off I thought, *Give me ninety days and I'll be all right.* That didn't happen, so I'm still in counseling. I go to counseling weekly.

Gaile will be on parole the rest of her life. If she needs to go out of Tennessee, she has to get permission and a travel permit from the parole officer. But parole is not hard for Gaile. She has to pay ninety dollars a month for the rest of her life, and, as she puts it, "The thing is, I get to pay the fee. That's what mercy looks like. That's how I look at it."

Gaile stops the conversation and looks right at me.

You know what else mercy looks like?

I get to drive and get stuck in standstill traffic.

I get to get wet from the rain going from one building to the other.

I get to walk in the park with my grandchildren.

All the things I couldn't imagine myself saying for twenty-seven years.

That's mercy!

. . .

When I think about Gaile and Dorris and Becca and Regina and Jennifer, I don't pretend to understand the trauma they have suffered and how it has and will affect them. Their stories, like ours, are unfinished. And I pray that mercy will continue to meet them at every point along the journey. As I pray for each of us. You and I might not have had an abusive relationship, we might not be prostitutes or drug addicts or inmates on death row, but in this way, our stories are all the same: We all need mercy.

And here's the thing: The act of showing mercy to others is vital and important and is what this announcement is ultimately inviting us to do—but the Beatitudes offer us a beautiful internal work as well as an external one. So as we wrestle with what mercy looks like in our lives, we need to start here, with showing mercy to ourselves. What voices are you are listening to? Is it your accuser, your abuser—or the voices in your own head? The voices that want to diminish you and say that you're not good enough? That what you can offer will never be enough? The voices that tell you you've really messed up, that say you are worthless and you will amount to nothing?

Those voices can be so loud. But we can quiet them—by having mercy on ourselves in the deepest places, by getting up and doing the things they are telling us not to do. We can silence the cynicism with belief and with mercy and with kindness to ourselves. Because so often the first work of mercy is personal— as we not only understand the divine mercy from God, who is eternally merciful, but accept his mercy and show it to ourselves. This is the only way to walk on with our heads lifted up.

In the Beatitudes, Jesus is offering us presence at the bottom of all things, and mercy is profound presence when we least expect it. At times we find ourselves in the aftermath of decisions and desperate choices that we've made, decisions and behaviors that have harmed not only us but the people around us. As Amy put it, "In the desperate need to survive, we just make decisions that make us not recognize ourselves."[13]

And it's at the point when we realize we can't fix what we've done that mercy leaps into action.

This is the very heart of the Beatitudes: that no matter what our poverty looks like—whatever is missing—mercy comes and taps us on the shoulder and invites us to keep going. And we take that next step changed forever. Once we're on the receiving end of mercy, we see the way the world works differently. We are able to look at one another's mistakes with more kindness and understanding and less judgment and offer mercy in return. Showing compassion and kindness for others even when it seems

like the impossible thing to do—the upside-down thing to do—
is the invitation here. Maybe we've been hurt by a friend's behavior or choices or words. But I'm reminded of these often-quoted
words: "Be kind, for everyone you meet is fighting a battle we
know nothing about."[14]

As we show mercy, we receive mercy. We enter the mercy
dance.

So maybe our story is not so different from those of the
women in this chapter.

Look at what they were handed:

Lives of abuse and betrayal.

And because that's what they were given, that's what they
passed on.

And then—

in their brokenness,

they were offered an overwhelming experience of mercy.

And because that's what they were given,

that's what they are passing on.

No one is beyond mercy's reach—not you, not me, not a
prostitute or drug addict, not an inmate on death row.

May mercy heal our hearts, lift our heads, and always be on
our lips as we offer it to others.

PURE IN HEART

The Wonder of It All

The journey to a thousand stars is not
too far a journey in the quest to have
true love abiding in a pure heart.

C. JOYBELL C.

• • •

Blessed are the pure in heart,
for they will see God.

MATTHEW 5:8

• • •

You're blessed when you get your
inside world—your mind and heart—put right.
Then you can see God in the outside world.

MATTHEW 5:8, MSG

• • •

With childlike eyes remade for wonder
And a heart that's undivided
I'm beginning to see you

"UNDIVIDED (PURE IN HEART),"
AMANDA COOK AND STU G

THERE'S A FAMOUS STORY that you've probably heard, but I'd like to tell it again.

So there was a father with two sons, and he owned land, and they farmed it together.

The younger son felt like he could have a better life and more adventure away from his dad and brother, and so he asked if he could have his share of the land that would eventually be his inheritance. It was a bit like saying, "I wish you *were* dead already"—very humiliating and painful for the father, who loved his boy.

Everything this father had was available to his sons, but this youngest couldn't see it.

He took his share of the land and turned it into cash. He went to a far-off country and blew it all on the pursuit of happiness—sex and good times.

A recession and severe famine hit the land that the son was in, and with his money and fake friends all gone, he offered himself to a local farmer, who sent him to feed his pigs—which for a Jew was degrading enough. But things got so bad, he hit rock bottom and was even ready to share the scraps of the pigs' food.

He finally came to his senses.

He decided to go home, but he would say to his father, "I've done you wrong. I'm not worthy to be your son—make me one of your hired hands."

So he left for home, and while he was still a long way off his father saw him in the distance and did something undignified and extraordinary: He ran to meet the boy. When he reached him, he hugged him tight and kissed him.

The boy said, "Father, I don't deserve to be your son—please take me as a hired hand."

The father was having none of it, and he told the servants to bring the finest clothes, a ring for his son's finger, and the best shoes. He also arranged to have the party of all parties—singing, dancing, and the best beef as a feast to welcome his son home.

The older son didn't go to the party; he was angry because his brother didn't deserve this kind of welcome. The father wondered where he was and went out to find him. "Come and celebrate—your brother is home," he said.

The older brother was furious: "All these years I've slaved away for you, done everything right, and obeyed your every word, and you never even gave me a goat so I could have a party with my friends."

"But, Son," the father said, "you've always been with me. Everything I have is yours. Don't you see? We have to celebrate and be happy—your brother was dead but has come alive again. He was lost but now is found."

We often see this story as a way to encourage those who feel lost and messed up and far away, that they are always welcome to come home to the family. That's a good thing.

But there's another way to see this.

The father is the star of this story. He is full of love and mercy and is always the same. He gave the boys the same treatment. They both got the land and the freedom to do whatever they wanted with it. The father's heart was always open, ready to forgive and restore no matter how great the failure. N. T. Wright likes to call this story "The Running Father" because of that extraordinary scene.

While the father's heart is open and ready to forgive—both the boys have a heart issue.

The younger gives his purity away to the wrong people and to instant self-gratification.

The elder son's heart issue is one of "doing the right things" at the cost of truly living and truly loving. He turned his home into a place of hard work without love and celebration.

Both of these heart issues stopped the sons from being able to *see* their father as he truly is: ever self-giving, always merciful, completely loving.

For the youngest son's heart to heal, he must fully embrace the forgiveness offered and realize he can't "work" to pay off any debt he feels he owes. He doesn't need to be a second-class citizen.

For the oldest son's heart to become whole, he needs to let go of his pride and judgment and misunderstanding of what being a son means. It would also be cool if he forgave his brother and gave up on the story that life is about being seen to "do the right things."

With love as the sole motive, maybe then their hearts would be pure and they could really see what their father is like.[1]

• • •

Can you "see" God?

That would sort a lot of stuff out, wouldn't it?

Even just to know for sure that the Holy One is there and real would be amazing, right?

The Teacher says that we'll see God if we have pure hearts. What does that mean? Isn't that impossible?

I say impossible because later on in the sermon, Jesus says that stuff about how even looking at someone and lusting after them is like taking them to bed. Or how being really angry with someone is as bad as murdering them.

Oh, how our hearts corrupt so easily. How my own heart corrupts so easily.

I'm pulled this way and that, and the rush is strong, especially when it's something that pushes boundaries—you know?—or is a little secret and a bit naughty.

Pure in heart? Not me!

Whenever I would hear this verse, I'd break out in a cold sweat. I'd feel like someone was watching me and just waiting for me to mess up. The voices would be there: "Who are you kidding? I know what you're really like." I'd want to run and hide because I know for sure that neither my heart nor my hands are clean.

Ever feel like we're all doomed? Or is it just me?

And once again I've missed the point. Jesus doesn't condemn and accuse. Instead he faces the accusers and says, "If you don't have any sin, then throw the first stone."

So what could be another way of understanding these words beyond what we come up with in our black-and-white, rule-making, "enlightened" minds?

It's so easy to beat ourselves up and forget the message at the core of the Beatitudes: that God is kindness and mercy—fully present with us when we least expect it. We're just not looking in the right place.

This is about giving ourselves a break, lifting our heads up, not staring at the ground in shame or trying to be pure or striving to be clean. Because as Chris Rea says, "Keep your head above the water, you get dirty and mean / Scrubbing forever and you never come clean."[2]

I like what Eugene Peterson says in *The Message*, and it gives us another clue as to what could be going on here: "You're blessed when you get your inside world—your mind and heart—put right. Then you can see God in the outside world" (Matthew 5:8).

So perhaps what Jesus is saying is about what is going on inside of us. All the stuff we keep hidden from the outside world and don't want anyone to see.

Perhaps this is about reconciling our insides with our outsides.

Perhaps this is about a divided heart. Maybe we have trouble seeing God if our hearts are not whole.

Richard Rohr often talks about the dualistic lives we all lead, as opposed to living with a unified and reconciled wholeness. We constantly wrestle with competing concepts such as life and death, and these things normally get reconciled on the deathbed. A contemplative lifestyle, like Rohr and his fellow Franciscans lead, helps us to reconcile these things a lot sooner in life, so we become more fully present and accepting of the life that is presented to us.

One of the things Rohr talks about is true self versus false self.

We all show the world a false self. This is the self I portray on Facebook, alongside the books, films, and music I want you to know I've read, watched, or listened to; my current successes; all the things I'm really good at.

Perception is everything.

I don't want you to look past the exterior. The true self, the real me, the person inside, would be a different story. I might be falling apart, struggling with all manner of decisions, behaviors, choices, addictions. I can say one thing and mean something else completely on the inside.

My psychologist friend Jim McNeish helped me understand it further. The heart becomes divided when we create a pride position—what we put on show when we are convinced of our "rightness."

When we create a pride position, we also create a shame position. When we were children, we experienced everything. When we were sad, we let ourselves feel sad, and when we were angry or happy, we let ourselves feel it and show it. But somewhere along the way, we were rejected and we felt shame, and we didn't want to feel shame, so we pushed it down—and that's when our heart divided.

In psychological terms, it's what is known as persona and shadow.

What if, when we read, "Blessed are the pure in heart," there's something else inside the text that we can pull out to help bring some freedom and innocence back into our lives? Something other than the feelings of guilt and shame, of never quite feeling good enough and constantly missing the mark?

There's a flow to these beatitude announcements. The previous announcement that invites us to show mercy means we receive mercy. God's mercy takes care of the things we want to hide. We can bring everything into the light of day in all its mess and all its chaos.

When we bring our shadows into the light, we can begin to put our hearts back together.

And if that is how we get to see God—by having a whole heart—I want that.

So how do we do this? Is it possible to regain our innocence once we've lived life a bit? Are we on the right track when we hold our failures and successes all together in one big muddly bag of life and present this to the universe?

For most of my Christian life I've been part of churches that would fall under the evangelical/charismatic banner. It's the way my journey unfolded, and I don't regret it. I'm proud to have been connected to some extraordinary people and movements, and it's made my story what it is. The last few years, though, I've been learning about different streams, about different religions and traditions, and there are some things that stand out as unique with regard to the contemporary evangelical/charismatic church. Such as the emphasis on a personal relationship with God (which I totally get, but it can become all about *me* and not about *us*), an emphasis on the emotional "experience" in worship and ministry, and a love of celebrity (we love our star preachers, teachers, and worship leaders). These things can make us either strive to be special or feel like we're not good enough.

And lurking just under the surface of our evangelical experience is the pressure of an unspoken list of rules and sins that would see us cast out should we fail. When someone implies that what I need is clean hands and a pure heart, or I hear the news that a friend or leader has "fallen," my mind tells me it can only be about sex or some other moral purity issue.

But in the Gospels, Jesus is never really mad at folks who've struggled with sexual things. He's concerned with transformation. In fact, the Bible is full of stories and characters who quite frankly wouldn't get a second chance in some churches today. Just look at King David!

C. S. Lewis said this:

If anyone thinks that Christians regard unchastity as the supreme vice, he is quite wrong. The sins of the flesh are bad, but they are the least bad of all sins. . . . According to Christian teachers, the essential vice, the utmost evil, is

Pride. Unchastity, anger, greed, drunkenness, and all that,
are mere fleabites in comparison: it was through Pride
that the devil became the devil: Pride leads to every other
vice: it is the complete anti-God state of mind.[3]

In the Gospels we see Jesus getting pretty tough with pride,
arrogance, and the way we keep people down with our knowledge, attitudes, rules, religion, power, and wealth.

He says to some religious leaders, "You burnish the surface of
your cups and bowls so they sparkle in the sun, while the insides
are maggoty with your greed and gluttony. . . . Scour the insides,
and then the gleaming surface will mean something" (Matthew
23:25-26, MSG).

Tough words, but hear the message. There's a disconnect
between the inside and the outside. When our actions and our
hearts are completely different, we have a divided heart, not a
whole heart. We all have the traits of a first-century Pharisee.

Brad Nelson says that the talk of pure hearts and seeing God
would have reminded the Jewish audience of Psalm 24:

Who can climb Mount GOD?
    Who can scale the holy north-face?
Only the clean-handed,
    only the pure-hearted;
Men who won't cheat,
    women who won't seduce.

PSALM 24:3-4, MSG

Jesus was using a few words to remind folks familiar with the
Scriptures of a larger story.

There were over six hundred purity laws in the first century, and every rabbi would have his own way of interpreting and following them—their *yoke*. If you wanted to be a disciple of a certain teacher, you had to meet that teacher's standard. You had to put on the yoke. If you couldn't live up to his interpretation of the purity codes, if you weren't seen doing the right things, you couldn't follow that rabbi. The outside was everything! The show had to be good. And in the same way, we can make our standards, our certainty, our black-and-whiteness an idol and nigh on impossible to live up to. This leaves a lot of people on the outside.

On the other hand, our Teacher—our rabbi on the hill—says, "My *yoke* is easy and my burden is light" (Matthew 11:30, emphasis added).

Richard Rohr tells us that oftentimes "in the Gospels, wherever you read 'sinners' it simply refers to the people who can't do it right—very often because they can't afford the Temple fees."[4]

I guess many in that context felt like failures. They didn't come up to the mark.

Just like I don't come up to the mark.

INNOCENCE LOST

I love children. Karen and I have two girls whom we've watched grow up into incredible, beautiful humans. In 2015 our older daughter and her husband had a beautiful daughter of their own and began that journey for themselves.

I'd guess that all of us who are parents have the stories of that dinner with friends when our toddler decided to climb out of bed, strip naked, and run into the room showing off and making everyone laugh. It's hard not to laugh with them. Young children don't care. There's no sense of shame or being in the wrong. They haven't yet learned to hide their feelings. They let themselves feel everything they experience, and experience everything they feel.

What's on the outside is the same as what's on the inside. It's kind of pure.

Pure in heart, you might say.

For us as parents, the early years with our kids, before they start acting the way we tell them to, are amazing to watch. They can throw the biggest tantrum one minute and the next be laughing hysterically or just snuggling in your neck.

And then we teach them how to behave, and they learn quickly by how *we* behave what *we* think is "acceptable" and what *we* think is good behavior. Our children are watching us and become like us. Whether we like what we see or not.

Kids start out with this beautiful innocence, and it doesn't matter how good or bad at being parents we are, we change that in our kids—forever.

Ultimately, this learned behavior can get so deep, becoming a part of us, that we become experts at knowing how to make anyone accept us. If we behave a certain way, we think that people will let us "in" or give us what we want. We can become so controlling and manipulative—but on the outside it looks like I'm just a great guy!

Somewhere along the way our insides have become disconnected from our outsides.

We have divided hearts.

How can we begin to make them whole again?

REDISCOVERING OUR SENSE OF WONDER

Maybe you've seen that commercial for a travel website where a garden gnome urges us to "go and smell the roses." What a shame that we have to be reminded to take time to stop, look, breathe deep, disconnect, and enjoy what's around us.

When our family moved to America, I was really surprised at how little holiday or vacation time people take here. Everyone seems to work *all* the time. It seems like the American dream doesn't come about by dreaming at all.

But I'm learning that it's the act of taking time, being attentive to what's around us, and allowing ourselves to experience the moments that can reconnect us with our sense of wonder that can help us be whole again.

My favorite movie of 2013 was Ben Stiller's *The Secret Life of Walter Mitty*. I love everything about this movie, from the story line to the sound track. Walter Mitty is a dreamer (and I totally identify with that part of his character). But the thing that resounds for me most is that, whether we are workaholics or serial dreamers, we need to stop missing what is, here and now, right in front of our faces. If only we look, pay attention, and respond to what's offered, we can really start to live.

On the movie sound track there's a song that I love called "Stay Alive" by José González that helps me remember:

> *There's a rhythm in rush these days*
> *Where the lights don't move and the colors don't fade*
> *Leaves you empty with nothing but dreams*
> *In a world gone shallow*
> *In a world gone lean. . . .*

There is a truth and it's on our side
Dawn is coming
Open your eyes.[5]

Stop and notice what's around.
Take a moment.

• • •

In 2007 Karen and I met Joseph Edelheit while having lunch
at a hotel in India. We were sitting there, taking in the beauty
and colors of the grounds as well as the delicious food, when a
guy who looked a lot like Jerry Garcia from the Grateful Dead
walked in and sat with us. He asked what I did, and I said I was
a musician. I asked what he did, and he said he was a rabbi.

I told him I'd just finished reading *Jewish Spirituality: A Brief
Introduction for Christians* by Rabbi Lawrence Kushner.

"Ha—Larry! He's a good friend!" said Rabbi Joseph in a
large and loud American voice. We talked for three hours that
day. I'm so glad we met. He has become such a great friend and
teacher to Karen and me.

Rabbi Joseph was there because he and his wife had raised
$100,000 to build an orphanage for HIV-positive children
in Chandrakal, near Hyderabad. All of the children had been
orphaned by AIDS. Karen and I visited, and over the years
since, those kids and Rabbi Joseph have inspired and taught
us so much.

After thirty years of being a synagogue rabbi, Joseph has
enjoyed an academic career as professor emeritus of religious and
Jewish studies at St. Cloud State in Minnesota, and also as a visiting professor at both pontifical and federal universities in Rio

de Janeiro, Brazil. Many years ago as a young man in seminary, Joseph studied under Rabbi Abraham Joshua Heschel. Rabbi Joseph delighted in introducing us to his mentor's work.

In his masterpiece book *The Sabbath*, Heschel talks about the holiness of time:

> One of the most distinguished words in the Bible is the word *qadosh*, holy; a word which more than any other is representative of the mystery and majesty of the divine. Now what was the first holy object in the history of the world? Was it a mountain? Was it an altar?
>
> It is, indeed, a unique occasion at which the distinguished word *qadosh* is used for the first time: in the Book of Genesis at the end of the story of creation. How extremely significant is the fact that it is applied to time: "And God blessed the seventh *day* and made it *holy*." There is no reference in the record of creation to any object in space that would be endowed with the quality of holiness.[6]

This invites me to read the "Moses and the burning bush" story differently. Moses was a shepherd for forty years. I don't really know, but he had probably seen bush fires before. He noticed that this bush was on fire but not burning up.

Moses takes time to investigate—and meets God.

Moses meets God in a moment of curiosity.

Moses hears God's voice in a moment of awe and wonder.

Jewish rabbis teach us that if we pay attention, if we take time, we can meet God in the moment. We can take off our shoes and say this ground is holy, but only if we take the time in that place.

We find God in time, in the moment. We can find him no matter what part of space we are in—and when we do, we find ourselves in the mystery of being connected to something far greater than ourselves.

MOMENTS

I first set foot in America in 1991. My pastor and a friend and I were travelling to Nicaragua to play some music and support a small church that was building a farm near the coastal harbor city of Bluefields. We had an overnight stop in Houston, Texas, and as we left the airport terminal building, walking out of the air-conditioning into the afternoon heat, I was taken aback by the humidity. All of a sudden the air was hot and thick like we were breathing through some kind of warm goo.

You have to remember it's not like that in the UK.

In my taken aback-ness I didn't at first notice the people who were also waiting curbside. I heard a voice that I recognized and looked to my right. Standing right there beside me was the British TV personality, botanist, and environmental campaigner David Bellamy, OBE.

David is a larger-than-life character, the sort who would appear on all kinds of TV shows from the news to children's shows talking about "beautiful flora and fauna" or his latest expedition. His distinctive voice was the butt of every comedic impersonator's gags.

While we were all waiting for a hotel shuttle (to give me something to think about other than jet lag and sweaty clothing),

I asked him what he was doing in Houston. He, like us, was only staying overnight, and he went on to tell me about the expedition he was on. He was taking ten Coca-Cola competition winners to his favorite bird-watching spot in the world, somewhere in the Brazilian rain forest.

He went on to talk about the expedition and what they would see, why it was his favorite spot, what he couldn't wait to discover, and what he was campaigning for environmentally in Brazil.

I was hooked! He was so passionate. Every word that came out of his mouth dripped with a sweet integrity and authenticity that made me feel like signing up straightaway and going with him.

It struck me then, and even more now looking back, how connected his words were to his heart—how unfiltered it was. How childlike it was.

How pure in heart it was.

• • •

In February 1996 my friend Jeff Searles was recording *Touching the Father's Heart (#27)* at the Anaheim Vineyard Church in California. The Cutting Edge Band (as Delirious? was known then) had helped Jeff record his album *Inside Me* the year before, and Jeff wanted me to play guitar on the Vineyard release.

So my second time in America was to come and play guitar. I fell in love with Southern California, the climate, the beaches, the tri-tip, the friends I made, Sunset Boulevard . . . the list goes on. To kids growing up in Britain back then, America meant Hollywood, the movies, Springsteen, astronauts, Nirvana. It was epic.

We had five hours free one day, so my friends took me to

Disneyland. We virtually ran round all the attractions until the *Fantasmic!* show over the lake at the end of the day before the fireworks.

I know I'm a sucker, emotional and easily impressed, but it gave me a feeling I hadn't experienced since I was a kid. A real visceral sense of wonder and excitement and delight. You know when you're at Grandma's house as a kid, and everything is so big, every room holds an adventure, and every closet holds a secret? It was like that.

My family were at home back on the south coast of England. Kaitlyn was five and Eden was nearly two. Our VHS (yes, it was the '90s) shelf was full of Disney movies. Kaitlyn's favorite was *Beauty and the Beast*. So when Mrs. Potts appeared projected onto a water fountain at Disneyland and sang "Tale As Old As Time" to her son, Chip the teacup, I'm not going to lie—I cried like a baby and promised myself (and later my girls) that I'd take them back there someday.

Which I did.

•   •   •

One more story.

The other day Karen and I were watching TV and saw an episode of *Undercover Boss*, where the president of an auto body shop company went undercover disguised as a trainee to meet his employees and see what it was like on the shop floor.

At the end of the show the boss revealed himself to the people who worked for him. One of the employees was a painter named Christian who was from Puerto Rico. He'd come to America with $1,300 two years before with his wife, who was now expecting their first baby. The boss was so impressed with

Christian's work quality and ethic, his story, and his life attitude despite all the hardship he'd experienced along the way.

The boss told him he wanted to:

- personally train him in business so he could have his own franchise
- have Christian develop a Spanish-speaking course for painters
- pay for all the grandparents to come visit the baby
- help pay Christian's rent for one year
- provide a $20,000 gift for him and his wife

Christian's reaction was priceless. So complete in its honesty and authenticity. Unexpected, extravagant kindness brought a moment of pure, unadulterated thanks and gratitude.

I saw God in that.

It wasn't the things Christian was given (although they were incredibly helpful). It was the moment.

So what do a botanist, my story at Disney, and an auto body shop painter have to do with a peasant teacher talking to a crowd on a hillside overlooking the Sea of Galilee?

Everything.

Because these are real human stories involving mystery and wonder and connecting to something greater.

I really believe in the human race—that it was a good idea. And because God's DNA lives in each and every one of us, I agree with Archbishop Desmond Tutu when he says that although most of the time the evil we see around us seems invincible, "ultimately right will prevail."[7] I believe that all of us are capable of experiencing moments when we regain our sense of wonder and awe and mystery.

Our sense of childlikeness.

LIKE A CHILD

It's important to remember that the people who wrote down the stories of Jesus included stories about children. Just think of all the stories Jesus must have told and all the things he did in his travels that they could have written about and remembered. But somehow these stories about children were important enough—sixty or so years after the events happened, in a culture where only men were really valued—to be included.

Matthew, Mark, and Luke all mention Jesus interacting with children. One of my favorite stories is this:

> At about the same time, the disciples came to Jesus asking, "Who gets the highest rank in God's kingdom?"
>
> For an answer Jesus called over a child, whom he stood in the middle of the room, and said, "I'm telling you, once and for all, that unless you return to square one and start over like children, you're not even going to get a look at the kingdom, let alone get in. Whoever becomes simple and elemental again, like this child, will rank high in God's kingdom. What's more, when you receive the childlike on my account, it's the same as receiving me."
>
> MATTHEW 18:1-5, MSG

So let's give ourselves a chance here. We don't have to be really, really clever.

These Beatitudes are not about us striving. They are announcements of how God works, where you'll find him, what it looks like where he is. The Beatitudes are not about the condition but about the Kingdom.

Rabbi Joseph tells me that it's like looking at the horizon—we may see the destination, but we're not there just yet. On the way we get chances to glimpse what it's going to be like.

A glorious not-yet-ness.

I like Rabbi Lawrence Kushner's phrase and book title *Eyes Remade for Wonder*. Remember how the heart divides when we take a pride position? When we are so certain of our rightness? My friend Jim McNeish told me that the opposite of rightness is curiousness. I like that. Too much certainty kind of scares me nowadays.

So maybe a good, nondualistic posture to take could be: "Speak, Lord. I'm listening."

Say it from a place of wonder and mystery and not knowing.

Will we ever be completely pure in heart? I don't think so. There's a lot against us. But there *will* be times when we'll get a glimpse of what it's like. Because in the moments when grace taps us on the shoulder and surprises us and we make time to notice, it will draw out the purest, most innocent, most wonder-filled responses, and maybe—just maybe—we'll glimpse what God is really like.

PEACEMAKERS

Living in the Contested Space

Violence is not getting us closer to a better future.

RONI KEIDAR

●   ●   ●

Blessed are the peacemakers,
for they will be called children of God.

MATTHEW 5:9

●   ●   ●

You're blessed when you can show people
how to cooperate instead of compete or fight.
That's when you discover who you really are,
and your place in God's family.

MATTHEW 5:9, MSG

●   ●   ●

Can you meet me in the middle where the light don't shine
Where there are no sides
Between you and I
Can you meet me in the middle cos we got to find
Find another way

"PEACEMAKERS," STU G AND PAUL MOAK

IT'S A BEAUTIFUL DAY. The Mediterranean sunshine is warm on the skin but not too hot. She walks out of her house and through the beautiful garden, home to flowers of different colors and head-turning aromas. Olive and almond trees, dotted about, offer welcome shade from the midday heat of summer. She pauses for a moment: *This never gets old.* The almond blossom against the deep blue sky is something to behold, as is the farmland that her family have owned for years.

It's not like we own the land, she thinks. *It's like the land owns us.*

It would have seemed an impossible dream to her ancestors scattered across the globe without a homeland in the not-so-distant past.

She carries on her way a few yards, then opens the door of the car, which springs to life with a single turn of the ignition.

The car ride is not too long, twenty minutes or so. The roads look as familiar as any coastal Mediterranean town. Familiar because nothing looks the same.

But there is something that distinguishes these roads from their relatives in southern Spain, Italy, or the Greek islands: the thick, solid concrete bus shelters that lead a double life.

The car could find this place by itself by now, the number of weekly visits it has made. She makes the turn into the parking lot and heads to the meeting point.

It's really hard to leave Gaza nowadays. You can only leave to receive medical attention. So she waits patiently while the unknown friend is checked for the three correct papers. One from Hamas, one from the Palestinian Authority, and finally the one from the Israeli authorities. Sometimes she can help with the Israeli permissions. The rest is out of her hands.

At first she doesn't know if the man walking towards her is

her friend or enemy. But they have the next hour and a half on the ride to the hospital to get to know each other. And this is why she does it.

Israeli Roni Keidar has her hope in peace and is committed to putting a human face on the suffering that conflict brings. Suffering that sees rockets made from lampposts fall on her farmland, indiscriminately killing workers who are like family to her. Suffering that sees 1.7 million people barricaded into a twelve-mile-by-twenty-mile "postage stamp" strip of land with hardly any resources being allowed in or out.

Roni is a peacemaker.

Making peace, one person, one car journey at a time.

• • •

It's early in the morning, and a different farmer steps out onto the hundred acres of hillside that his grandfather bought a hundred years ago. The ancient arable terraces falling down the hillside, once full of vegetables and produce, now lay vacant and stony. Lying in wait, anticipating a new day when water once again flows onto the property.

He looks over the hundreds of trees that produce a harvest of olives, figs, almonds, and other fruits. Green leaves against a blue sky. He is grateful that they faithfully provide for his family despite the lack of a water supply.

He chuckles at the dogs chasing each other, making a racket around the tree where the long-suffering donkey, tied up in the shade, looks on as if to say, "Grow up." The only protest he shows is a swish of the tail and a resigned glance of the eyes.

The donkey, and the farmer, have seen a lot of change in the last twenty-five years. The settlements surrounding the hill have grown into towns, and only the fact that the farmer's grandfather obtained some paperwork to say he legally bought and registered the land with the Ottomans, and then the British, allows him to go to the courts and stand firm against the Authority's insistence that this is state land and should belong to the state.

It's a beautiful, rich land, and even though he has the papers to say it's his, *it's not like the land belongs to us*, he thinks. *It's like we belong to the land.*

For this moment in time, it's his responsibility to care for and nurture this piece of earth.

So he checks the underground cisterns that collect the rainwater, the solar panels that provide just about enough energy to survive, and the development of the caves that his ancestors lived in; because he can't get permission to build aboveground, he expands the farm the only way he can.

The military blocked the access roads in 2001, but that doesn't stop visitors from all over the globe, and best of all, it doesn't stop the children from coming. Jews, Arabs, Europeans, Americans— they help harvest, paint stones, create colorful murals in mosaic tile, because this is a beautiful story of a beautiful farm. The Tent of Nations.

When the military came and destroyed hundreds of fruit trees, this farmer invited the nervous young soldiers in for a cup of tea. He will plant new trees, because this Palestinian farmer refuses to be a victim, refuses to hate, refuses to be an enemy.

Daoud Nassar is a peacemaker.

Making peace one tree, one cup of tea, one group of children at a time.

• • •

The pilgrim hurries his morning coffee, and with taste buds buzzing with the strong memory of arabica and cardamom, he begins to trace the steps he's walked every day for the last week. He's five thousand miles from the place he calls home, but relishing every second with a mixture of gratitude, struggle, and necessity. He's here because of what he had to offer, but with every minute and every step, another reason, another story is beginning to unfold.

Each day since arriving, he's journeyed along the same stones and alleys, reliving each day's feelings and memories late into the night, anticipating the next day. And it's something he's compelled to do in solitude. It's *his* journey and *his* story to own.

This shouldn't shock anyone else, except this pilgrim has not enjoyed his own company for a while. For many years his sense of value and worth has come from what he can do, what he can offer, who his friends are, what songs he can write, what concerts he can perform. Now a big part of that life is over, and he found himself with a hole he can't fill and an itch he can't scratch. There's a power that twists and turns and manipulates and never settles in the shadowy secret places of the soul, and there have been only illusions of help, temporary relief.

But this journey, these streets, these stones are different. They hold something special and sacred. He's accepted their invitation because every day they are pulling him, drawing him, inviting him to come with everything he has. "Bring it all," they say, so he loads up his internal baggage, bursting at the seams, and walks in solitude.

It's like wading through a river of ancient whispers, sending them out like ripples with every tread. The whispers bounce off the walls, echoing back their approval: "Keep going, friend. It's worth it."

He thinks of the life he has been given, his successes and failures and hopes for the future.

"This life does not belong to you," the stones say. "You belong to this life."

At the very top of Star Street, there is a square where the cafés and bazaars once bristled and buzzed with economic energy. Color and diversity filled the place—but a wall was built, and it diverted the flow of life elsewhere. In recent years the color and energy have left. That is, until last weekend, when a festival of music, art, and culture brought life back into Star Street. Cafés and stores opened once again, people sweeping the floors and painting their walls in anticipation of the thousands who would come and celebrate, bringing a brief but sweet relief to this part of town.

Our pilgrim took part, invited by good friends doing great work. He did not know what he would find there, but it was a much-needed adventure. What he discovered amid the symphony of dead things coming to life was a hunger and thirst for the same to happen in his own deepest places. For color and life to burst out of the shadow.

All the talk of security and walls and separation felt familiar. Somewhere along the way he discovered a wall in his own heart, separating, discriminating, polarizing, creating a hunger for wholeness. He couldn't get around it, he couldn't get over it, and the worst thing was how it was affecting others.

Today, when he reaches Manger Square, he doesn't make the usual stop for the customary "best falafel in Bethlehem," followed by another coffee fix. Today he keeps walking, spinning as he crosses the square, taking in the scenery, fine-tuning the sensory perception. He will be leaving town soon and wants to make the most of every moment.

He keeps going, crosses the road, and, through an opening in the crusader wall, enters the Church of the Nativity. *There will be hundreds in here*, he thinks, but inside there are no lines leading underground to the place where tradition says this baby was born. So he follows the shiny and grooved path of the millions of pilgrims before him and climbs down the steps.

There's an understandable sprinkling of religious artifacts down here, but it's easy to see what it's like without them: simple, a dark cave, once part of a home where animals were kept safe.

At the spot where the manger is thought to have been, our pilgrim stops moving. There's a prickling sense that this journey, the point of this story, has been coming to this moment.

He kneels in silence, but his brain is not silent.

More than I want anything else in the whole world, I want this story to be true. More than I need anything else in the whole world. If you are the Prince of Peace, in this place where you were born, where you were made flesh, I need you to come alive again on the inside of me.

There are no visions or flashes of lightning, no appearance of angels, not really any feelings at all apart from the desire of the prayer itself, but somewhere in a deep place a crack appears in the wall and lets a little light shine into the shadows.

In years to come our pilgrim will look back on this moment, knowing that a new chapter has begun—because Stu Garrard is a peacemaker, and he has learned that you can't begin to give peace to others in the world until you first receive peace as a gift on the inside.

PEACE: THE IMPOSSIBLE DREAM?

As I've said before, I really hate confrontation. I don't like violence or fighting talk. I've never punched anyone in anger, although I for sure have deserved a punch or two along the way.

All that to say, this announcement, "Blessed are the peacemakers, for they will be called children of God" (Matthew 5:9), is one of the most compelling and confronting and important announcements in the Sermon on the Mount.

We all feel like this. When we are confronted with violence and conflict, we just want to hit back with more violence. We must get our own back. This plays out personally, and it plays out with military and governments. We think we are putting the world to rights when we respond with greater force. But, as Walter Wink says, the idea of redemptive violence is a myth. When Jesus says, "But I tell you, do not resist an evil person. If anyone slaps you on the right cheek, turn to them the other cheek also" (Matthew 5:39), he's not telling us to submit to evil, but to refuse to oppose it on its own terms.[1]

This is hard and subversive stuff.

In the early 2000s, Delirious? played a show somewhere in Texas, and at the meet and greet we met a couple of loud young guys wearing cowboy hats. They couldn't wait to tell us that they had just returned from serving in Iraq and that as the U.S. forces rolled into Baghdad for the first time, they were blasting our song "History Maker" from their tank.

I found myself speechless. I just didn't know what to say, and so I didn't say much at all. Such a mixture of emotions and thoughts. I had my own doubts about and my own ignorance of that war, and I had no idea of the terrible things these young men had seen or the terrible things they had been made to do in the line of duty. So I showed my appreciation of their service.

But I couldn't believe that our song had been used like that. "History Maker" is not a war song. It's about joining God in his work of redeeming and renewing all creation. Making things whole . . . not blasting them apart.

The biblical word we translate in English as "peace" is *shalom*. We looked at this word before when we talked about hunger and thirst. *Shalom* means a kind of wholeness, nothing missing, nothing broken, everything in its right place between us and God, us and each other, us and the earth.

Blessed are the wholeness-makers.

Blessed are the shalom-makers.

It's internal and it's external.

In the early Roman Empire, Caesar was the one who brought peace. He wanted to be known as the son of a god, and he brought peace by fear, terror, and the most extreme violence by the use of his military superpower.

Time and again in the Gospels we see Jesus, the Son of God, bringing peace in a different way. Peace through a different kind of power.

At the time he was arrested, Jesus rebuked Peter for drawing his sword and cutting off the ear of the high priest's servant. It must have been a mighty swing! Peter wanted to protect Jesus with all his might, but Jesus told him, "All who draw the sword will die by the sword" (Matthew 26:52). And he healed the wound.

He allowed himself to be taken away and executed, even forgiving those who carried out the most awful death penalty.

So what does this mean for us? How can we be people who

follow Jesus in how we make peace? How do we live as shalom bringers?

It may seem a surprise that I am choosing to base this chapter in one of the most difficult and painful locations of conflict on the planet: the Holy Land, the location of the Israeli-Palestinian conflict. I am not an expert. This chapter is *not* about the historical, religious, and political context. That is impossibly, deeply complicated. As we look at this idea of peacemakers, we want to look not at the *why* but at the *how*. How can we be peacemakers in a world where there is so little peace?

SHABBAT SHALOM

The best of times happen around meals, a full table, connecting, sharing life, and telling stories. One of my most memorable was on a Friday night in England with Rabbi Joseph and some friends in our home. Karen had prepared an incredible feast, and because it was Shabbat, we asked Rabbi Joseph to lead us through some traditional Jewish prayers and blessings. I'll never forget him starting with the *shalom aleichem* and the *kiddush*, the blessing of the wine. We felt beautifully connected to a story so much larger than us.

When I told Rabbi Joseph that I was going to the Holy Land, he said, "You have to experience Shabbat in the holiest city on the holiest night."

Which I did.

My fellow travelers and I were welcomed into the home of Hadas and Gidon Melamed and their children, a young Orthodox Jewish family. It was a beautiful highlight of my time in Jerusalem. We sang, we ate, we listened, we watched. It filled our bellies; it filled our souls.

In Bethlehem, on another day, I became friends with a Palestinian Muslim, Abdelfattah Abusrour. I had visited his work at Alrowwad, a centre for culture and the arts in Aida refugee camp. I wanted to spend more time with him and learn more about his work of nonviolent resistance, and he immediately invited me to dinner that night. Again, it was a night I will never forget, sitting around the table with his family, learning of their culture and listening to their stories. Incredible hospitality and food, and one of his sons, through much laughter, taught me how to play the oud.

Eating meals is nice, but the bigger picture is about the people and their stories. I'm a listener. And in this land, with the people who have suffered here, I'm treading carefully and respectfully.

These words from the hill were spoken on this very piece of earth. It's where my journey has taken me, it's where I discovered the need for a first step of peace to be born on the inside, and it's where I've found this announcement being worked out in flesh and blood.

So with heart and hands open, it's time to meet some people who can teach us a little about what it looks like to make peace.

Todd Deatherage

In 2013 I was invited by the Amos Trust and Greenbelt Festival to take part in the inaugural Bet Lahem Live Arts Festival in Bethlehem. I jumped at the chance. And after the festival, I stayed on for another week to join a group of musician friends on a trip with another hero of mine, Todd Deatherage, and his organization, the Telos Group. Todd spent ten years on Capitol Hill in Washington, DC. During his time there, he worked in the Senate as a chief of staff, in the Bush administration human rights bureau, and in the policy-planning office of the State Department under Condoleezza Rice. Todd pursued his interest in international human rights issues, and while working for the government, he quickly became aware of how much power the United States has in the world—and the responsibility that comes with that.

The United States projects a lot of power. Diplomatic power, military power, economic power. Todd says, "Because of that, we don't have the luxury of not knowing about things because we have the responsibility to use that power in the best ways we possibly can."[2] Todd is a Christian who doesn't want to compartmentalize his faith but wants to live it out in the public square and articulate it in ways that are advancing a common good.

His human rights work led him to religious issues all over the Middle East, and as time went on, people whom he was meeting and working with began talking about the Israeli-Palestinian issue. He decided to visit the Holy Land to see for himself what was going on.

He met a guy named Greg Khalil, a member of an international group of lawyers advising the Palestinian Authority, and he spent a week meeting people on both sides of the conflict who were working on finding a way forward after the Oslo Accords.

This was a whiplash moment for Todd as a Christian. He began to realize that particularly the evangelical church in America, which has a huge voice in the political picture of any government, wasn't having the opportunity to hear all the narratives from Israel and Palestine. It dawned on him that if we have a blanket support of one side or another—theologically, politically, or otherwise—we are just importing that conflict into our own culture.

When the Bush administration came to an end and Todd was about to take another job, Greg asked him what it would look like to form an NGO that would educate American leaders, Christians, and others about the conflict in ways that help and support peacemaking. Todd immediately said, "Not only do I support you, I want to help you."

And that's how the Telos Group was born: a pro-peace organization whose banner reads, "Pro/Pro/Pro Peacemaking."

So there I was with a bunch of people in Jerusalem, some I knew and others I didn't. Shell-shocked by the stories and experiences of the previous week. The Telos week was to start in the same shocking way: in Jerusalem at Yad Vashem, the Holocaust memorial and museum.

I was not unfamiliar with Jewish history, because Rabbi Joseph has educated me on the Diaspora and the Holocaust. But Yad Vashem left me speechless. I will never forget it.

And so the week went on: a whole day of Israeli perspectives, a whole day of Palestinian perspectives, meals with Orthodox Jewish families, another refugee camp in the West Bank, a meeting with a sheik to learn about Islam in the Holy Land. We met with Palestinian Christians and Muslims. I got to know peacemakers of all kinds: activists, professors, rabbis, farmers, business folk, and families living every single day with checkpoints and the struggles and difficulty of the conflict.

It's a strange pilgrimage. One of visiting sacred spaces, treading carefully so as not to disturb anyone's contemplation, walking your own spiritual pilgrimage, and being shaken to the core because "I had no idea it was like this."

I have learned so much from Todd about what it means to be a peacemaker. About desiring to walk a different path, a third way, rather than taking this side or that side. About being a listener no matter how competing or irreconcilable the stories are. About not buying into the cycle of violence and revenge, of cynicism, hopelessness, injustice, and despair—but working towards creating a *new* narrative, a narrative for mutual flourishing, for a common good.

As a friend of mine once said, "Good luck with that."

I mean, give me a guitar and I'll play you something. But peacemaking in one of the world's hot spots? I feel so unqualified. But the people I've met and the friends I've made are teaching me. Teaching me every single day by the way they wake up and carry on. Choosing a narrow way of forgiveness and reconciliation in the middle of their immense personal loss and suffering. The way of the Beatitudes . . . the way of Jesus.

Robi Damelin

Robi is a firecracker of a human being. An Israeli living in Tel Aviv, and formerly an executive in PR and advertising, Robi is a real go-getter, full of life. But her life changed tragically when in 2002 her son David was killed by a Palestinian sniper while guarding a checkpoint in the West Bank. He was studying philosophy of education at Tel Aviv University when he was called up as an officer on reserves. He didn't want to go and serve in the occupied territories but ultimately decided not to resist the obligation to serve in the military. "I was filled with dread," Robi says.

When the army came to tell Robi her son had been

murdered, the first words out of her mouth were "You may not kill anyone in the name of my child."

Robi says she understood very soon after that terrible day that the sniper didn't kill David because he was David. "If he'd have known him, he wouldn't have killed him," she says. As a young man, David's killer had watched his uncle be violently killed and had chosen the path of revenge. That day, it was David's turn to be in the way, along with nine others.

In her grief Robi came to the place of understanding that revenge would not bring David back. Even though she wakes up every day and for a moment wonders if it has all been a bad dream—before the gut-wrenching truth hits her again—the reality is that violence would just create more violence.

Because of Robi's work in PR and advertising, the media wanted to interview her and get her story. She was compelled to be an advocate for peace from the beginning, even though she was devastated by her loss.

The Parents Circle–Families Forum (PCFF)—a joint Palestinian-Israeli organization of over six hundred families who have lost close family members as a result of the prolonged conflict—reached out to her, and her story took another turn.

When she met Palestinian mothers who had also lost children, she knew they shared a common grief. The Parents Circle became her lifeline and the focus of her energies. Since joining she has worked tirelessly for coexistence, peace, and reconciliation. As spokesperson for the Parents Circle, Robi often travels and lectures to students and at events all over the world—usually alongside a bereaved Palestinian friend like Bassam Aramin, who lost his ten-year-old daughter when she was shot by an Israeli border guard.

When you listen to Robi talk, you feel the weight of daily choices she makes to be a peacemaker because, as she says, "This pain never leaves you."

There have been many tests along the way, like the next time the army knocked on her door and said they had captured the man responsible for David's murder. Robi thought to herself, *Am I being honest and do I mean what I say about reconciliation? Do I* really *mean what I'm saying?*

After agonizing over it and lying awake for many nights, she wrote the sniper's family a letter, telling them about David and the reconciliation work she is doing with Israelis and Palestinians, with the hope that one day they could meet. Years later, a letter came from the sniper in response, justifying his violence and David's death. "But I was free," Robi says. "I was no longer a victim dependent on the Palestinian sniper. The path of reconciliation brought peace to my life."

When I recently met up with Robi and listened to her story for the sixth time, she said, "You again? I thought you'd have had enough of me by now." But I am fascinated by her courage and strength, and I'll never get tired of hearing stories like hers.

When Robi talks about forgiveness, it disarms you. She looked me right in the eyes. "Could you forgive?" she said, and for a moment I felt like I was being interrogated while attached to a lie detector. Just for a moment, her eyes gave me a glimpse into her life of immense pain and determination. Then she broke into her cheeky smile and gave me an "I'll see you next time" kiss on the cheek.[3]

Sami Awad

Just a few hundred feet from the archway that was the only way into Bethlehem from Nazareth in the first century is a 250-year-old house that is currently home to an organization called Holy Land Trust. Sami Awad is the founder and director of the organization that, as their website says,

> through a commitment to the principles of nonviolence, . . . aspires to strengthen and empower the peoples of the Holy Land to engage in spiritual, pragmatic and strategic paths that will end all forms of oppression. We create the space for the healing of the historic wounds in order to transform communities and build a future that makes the Holy Land a global model for understanding, respect, justice, equality and peace.[4]

Sami is Palestinian, a Christian, and a peacemaker.

He says that if you ask a Jew, Christian, or Muslim who lives in this land to give it a name other than a political or historical name like Palestine or Israel, most would actually call it "Holy Land." He sees the name as common between them. He says that if we believe this is Holy Land, sacred land, then in a sense it doesn't belong to any of us—rather, it belongs to the Creator. This means to Sami that "those of us who live on this land should act as trustees of the land. We are to maintain and take care of it. We are to make it prosper; ultimately we are to make it a global symbol of peace. The world thinks this conflict cannot be resolved. Imagine when we do resolve it what the world will think then!"[5]

Looking around his office and seeing pictures of Martin Luther King Jr. and Gandhi, I asked him who his heroes are, thinking I already knew the answer.

"My grandmother," he said, "and my uncle." I was intrigued and asked him to explain.

It's the story of my grandma and her children and what happened to them as the result of the 1948 war. My grandmother and grandfather lived in Jerusalem with their children before 1948, and they lived in an area right outside the Old City. It was an area, like many areas in what was known as Palestine before 1948, where Jews, Christians, and Muslims all lived next to each other in the same neighborhood. This reality changed for my family when the war broke out and there was a lot of shooting and shouting in the area they were living in. My grandfather tried to protect his family by raising a white flag on top of his house to show both sides that, though they were fighting, there were civilians living there. And as he did that, he was shot by a sniper bullet and killed.

A few days after that, Sami's grandma and her children were evicted from their home and became part of the refugee population. So in a matter of days she lost her husband, her house, their property and possessions, their neighbors. With one bag and six children, she made her way to Bethlehem because she had a brother who was pastoring a local church there.

She couldn't afford to look after the children, so they ended up in an orphanage back in Jerusalem. Sami's father grew up there, able to see his old house from the orphanage.

Sami's grandmother instilled in the children that they were not to engage in revenge or retaliation. She said that their Christian faith called them to be peacemakers—but she told them at the same time not to remain silent in the face of injustice and to engage proactively in peace and reconciliation. "That was the seed my grandmother planted in her family many years ago," says Sami.

His grandmother passed away a few years ago now, and one thing she kept repeating all through her life was "I don't want you to find out who killed my husband, who did this to us, because if that person knew my husband, he wouldn't have pulled the trigger. So we need to forgive them and move on."

"We call her a saint," Sami says.

As a young boy, Sami's dad was sponsored by a visiting couple from the United States who fell in love with him and decided to pay for all his expenses and education. It was a one-in-a-million chance for this young Palestinian. After he graduated, the couple took him to the United States, where he continued his education and eventually became a U.S. citizen. On a visit back to the Holy Land he met Sami's mother, and they eventually moved to Kansas, where Sami was born.

When Sami was six months old, the family moved back to Bethlehem, as Sami's dad was offered a job to run an orphanage. That's where Sami grew up—in the orphanage with his parents and the orphaned children.

This was in the 1970s, after the 1967 war and the military occupation of the Palestinian territories. Life was difficult, and Sami as a young boy was wrestling with his family's insistence of working for peace when all he could see was people not wanting peace. And this is where his uncle comes into the story.

Sami's uncle was also a U.S. citizen and had been living in the States. The world was only hearing about Palestinians as terrorists, so Sami's uncle started a centre in Jerusalem to teach nonviolence. Sami found a place to express himself while remaining true to his family's ethic. From the age of twelve years old, Sami has been actively participating in the work of nonviolence and peacemaking.

His first demonstration was to plant trees on some land that was about to be confiscated, and for the first time he met Israeli peace activists who were helping the cause for peace. That meeting really helped Sami break the stereotype of what he thought he knew of Israeli society.

The peace movement grew through the first and largely nonviolent intifada (uprising). Though his work was definitely nonviolent, Sami's uncle got deported because he was mobilizing a lot of people in terms of protest and activism and was seen as a security threat.

Sami says, "My father was worried about me because I was starting to organize some student union activities and other peace protests. He didn't want me to get in trouble like my uncle did, so he decided to deport me." He laughs. "I found myself on a plane to America to continue my education."

Sami got a graduate degree in political science and a master's degree in peace and conflict resolution at the American University in Washington, DC. He returned to Bethlehem in 1996 not to work in nonviolence, but to work for peace. The Oslo Accords had recently been agreed upon, and there was a lot of hope for a peaceful two-state solution. Unfortunately, it didn't really work out like anyone hoped. With huge failures on all sides and things getting desperate, Sami said to some friends,

"We have to do something." The Holy Land Trust (HLT) was created in 2000—the same year as the second and extremely violent intifada started.

Sixteen years after he started HLT, Sami's commitment to the way of peace through nonviolence is stronger than ever. He talks a lot about transformation and has helped to put flesh on the bones of that language through starting the Bet Lahem Live Festival. "We had twenty-five thousand visitors in 2015," he delights in telling me. I'm sure the hotels and the shop owners were delighted too.

The Holy Land Trust runs workshops and training seminars for both Palestinians and Israelis, and they invite people from all over the globe to come and immerse themselves in life in the Holy Land.

I see a look of exasperation on his face at times when he gets asked political questions. "Our work is not political," he says:

> We don't really care what it looks like in the end—one state or two states. I recognize that a political solution is ultimately necessary, but that solution will have to honor the values of equality, dignity, and respect for all the communities, and that is what we do—that is what we are working for. Nonviolence is the *only* option, and this is what we teach. Many people say this is impossible, but I am looking for leaders who will have a vision for making the impossible possible. As a Palestinian, my life changed when I visited Auschwitz and Birkenau in Poland with some Jewish friends. I was not a Holocaust denier, but I got a sense of the trauma of a whole nation. Those who survived the worst expressions of the utmost evil,

the utmost violence, have survived with a great fear. That knowledge, that experience was truly life changing.

As a Christian, Sami is also engaging the question "How do I really bring the teachings of Jesus to this work? The man who said, 'Love your enemies' and 'Pray for those who persecute you.' The one who forgave his own executioners! Jesus didn't come to point to the past and condemn, but he came to transform and create a new future."

WHAT ABOUT THE REST OF US?

Many of us do not face conflict like Roni and Daoud and Robi and Sami. Their lives in one of the most intense hot spots on the planet look very different from ours.

One of the dangers of telling stories like these is that as humans we tend to turn people like these into saints. If we make these people into saints, we're subtly letting ourselves off the hook of embodying peacemaking in our own lives.

They're risking their lives in one of the most volatile, dangerous conflict zones in the world. Clearly, they've attained a kind of Christlikeness we ourselves aren't capable of. Right?

And yet the very people we're so quick to label as heroes are very often the ones insisting they've done nothing heroic. They simply did what anyone else in their shoes would have done had they been standing there. They saw a need and responded to what was in front of them by doing what they could to help. They saw conflict, and instead of ignoring it or stuffing it or pretending it wasn't there, they moved toward it. And that's ultimately what making peace is all about. Because the truth is, no matter where you are, we all build walls in the contested spaces in our lives.

The "how" for them is the same "how" for us.

Peacemaking is a difficult path.

Sometimes we have to step from behind our walls and onto the land where the rockets fall. Sometimes we have to walk into that emotional minefield.

Often we think it's easier to just carry on, so we keep peace instead of making it.

But striving to simply keep the peace is a huge mistake. The shalom of which Jesus speaks is not simply the absence of conflict. Shalom is much more profound. Shalom is everything as it should be. Everything in its place. A delicate and intricate interdependence. Which is to say, in order for me to be fully me, I need you to be fully you. If I am diminished, you are diminished. If you are diminished, I am diminished.

Shalom is about not the absence of conflict but, as Todd Deatherage would say, the presence of mutual flourishing. Mutual flourishing is about a resounding peace in which everything is in its right place.

Peacemaking is not peace-talking or peace-loving or peace-keeping. Peacemaking costs us.

Peacekeepers stay behind the walls. They walk on eggshells, they don't interact with people who believe differently, and all they ever get is what they currently have. They are not walking towards a better future.

Peacemakers, on the other hand, must engage others in order to make peace.

You have to listen.

What you desire for yourself is what you desire for others, no matter your differences.

You must walk from behind your walls and into the conflict zone to create a future that's different from what we have now.

And we all have conflict zones.

• • •

In the early days their love came easily. They'd go for walks, take trips together. Then came kids and careers and financial pressure. For the first time in their marriage they found themselves arguing about money. Soon they were arguing about who did what around the house, which morphed into fights about pretty much anything. With each new conflict, they entrenched themselves more deeply against each other, universalizing their anger with statements like "You always do this!" or "You never listen!" Gradually, a gap began to grow between them as they both learned how to stay out of each other's way. It was just easier. Now they're firmly stuck behind their fortifications, watching the other person's every move across this vast contested space. Their marriage has become a demilitarized zone, and to venture out from behind their walls and actually move towards each other would be to enter a no-man's-land littered with thousands of old hurts that could blow up at any moment. It won't be easy. It will be costly, but they each know the only way for healing to come is for them to step out from behind their walls and start moving towards each other. And as they do, they stop keeping peace and start making it, and the words from the hill hang somewhere between them: "Blessed are the peacemakers."

• • •

She'd built her team over many years and instilled a passion and vision that made it feel more like a family than staff, more like a movement than a business, and she was the talk of the town. But things had felt a little different just lately. Something had got stuck, and the business wasn't moving forward as it had been. There was discord in the team. After some investigation, she discovered that one of them, one of her closest friends, had been working behind her back and seizing the opportunity to use what they had built together for his own gain. It was like a dagger to her heart.

What was she to do? She wanted to say nothing, keep the peace, and hope it would pass. She dug out her notes from her leadership coach.

- What am I committed to?
- What am I passionate about?
- What is my unique contribution?
- What am I willing to suffer for?

If she brought this into the light, he could lose his job. If she did nothing, it could destroy the story and bring all they had worked for down in a crumbling mess.

In that moment her commitment to a better future seemed worth the risk, and she walked out from behind her defenses and into the frostiness with forgiveness and not revenge in mind. And the words from the hill whispered, "Blessed are the peacemakers."

• • •

He looked back on their friendship and smiled. So much shared history. Inseparable through high school and college, sharing each other's successes and failures.

"I got your back," he remembered saying when his friend had told him of his family's destruction due to his alcoholic father.

At the occasional drunken frat party, he had made sure his friend got back to the room safe and sound. "I got your back," he would say again.

Life had offered different career paths, and they continued to be close friends.

But just recently there had been a little more distance and a little less interaction. Long working hours and mood swings had caused his friend's girlfriend to end the relationship, and his friend couldn't handle it. It had ripped the Band-Aid off his abandonment and codependency issues, and the smell of whiskey on his breath was becoming a permanent aroma.

So he decided to go and visit, and when he did, he noticed the empty antidepressant containers alongside the empty whiskey bottles in the trash.

It would be easier to say nothing, turn a blind eye, slap him on the back, and keep the peace. But what kind of future would that bring?

The alternative would be risky—walk onto the battlefield and tell his friend he doesn't want to see him become like his father. He could be an agent of disruption to the cycle of self-violence and harm.

And the words from the hill are speaking still: "Blessed are the peacemakers."

• • •

In these words from the hill, our Teacher announces that

- when you walk from behind the walls of safety and onto dangerous ground,
- when you are prepared to put all at risk for the cause of mutual flourishing,
- when you become agents of disruption in the cycle of violence and harm,

God is with you.
God is on your side.

8

PERSECUTED
Holy Troublemakers

What are the things we do that are worth persecuting?
CLARENCE JORDAN

• • •

Blessed are those who are persecuted because
of righteousness, for theirs is the kingdom of heaven.
MATTHEW 5:10

• • •

You're blessed when your commitment to God
provokes persecution. The persecution drives you
even deeper into God's kingdom.
MATTHEW 5:10, MSG

• • •

When the world needs a hero
Can you be the hero
When the world needs a miracle
Can you be the miracle, you be the miracle
Safe and sound inside our bubble
But when the world needs to change
Can you make a little trouble? Can you make a little trouble?
"HOLY TROUBLEMAKERS," PROPAGANDA, STU G, PAUL MOAK

EARLIER TODAY I read about young Syrian Christians deciding not to flee the country, but to stay in Syria even though their lives are threatened.[1] It's hard to imagine the suffering they face, but they stay because their faith compels them to. Whatever the cost.

In January 2016, I read about attacks in Burkina Faso, where six of twenty-nine people who died were there doing humanitarian work because of their Christian faith, and a seventh man who was killed was a missionary. He and his wife had run an orphanage and a women's refuge there since 2011.[2]

Then I read about 2 million people, many of them Christians, who are being forced to leave their homes in northern Nigeria.[3] It sounds as if groups like Boko Haram and Hausa-Fulani are trying to carry out their own brand of ethnic cleansing—to eradicate Christianity.

These are the sorts of things that come to my mind when I read the persecution beatitudes. But is it really always "those people over there"?

You know what I mean?

The ones in other countries.

The ones who are losing their lives and homes.

What about us?

My story is so different. I don't really know what persecution looks like. I mean, I grew up with ginger hair and freckles, so I had a bit of name-calling, a bit of bullying, and one time, the most beautiful girl in the school walked over . . .

It was 1977. Yes, I was ginger, but I also had braces. My teeth were covered in enough metal to fence in a football field, and to be honest with you, I was struggling a bit back there. Especially whenever it was lunch break at Orwell High School, out there on the windy eastern edge of England. We'd just moved there as a family, and I was the new kid in the playground. I was all flares, big collars, and long ginger hair whipping around in the wind as I hung awkwardly about on the edge of the action, hoping to join in the lunchtime football game. I'd been there for a few weeks, and still nobody had called me over. I was beginning to doubt myself.

Then *she* came over. The most beautiful girl I'd ever seen. This was my Galadriel moment, as the vision that was Susan Miller materialized on the other side of the football pitch. I'd not been at the school long, but I'd been there long enough to know that Susan Miller was the girl every boy in the school fancied. She was the one, the only one. Nobody had as much confidence, shorter skirts, or bigger hair. And as I stared, I could have sworn that she was looking at me.

And she was.

Then something amazing happened. She started walking towards me. Like Moses leading the Israelites across the Red Sea, Susan Miller sliced her way through the football match, her handful of wannabes pouting just a few paces behind her.

As the football players realized that the object of their pubescent ache was heading over to the new kid, they, too, stopped and stared. Finally, like an orchestra called to silence by the conductor, the playground was ready for Susan Miller to speak to me.

She had stopped just a few steps in front of me, close enough that I could smell her apple-scented hair spray, far enough so she had to raise her voice so everyone could hear.

"You're the new boy, aren't you?"

"Yes."

"I know your name."

I blushed. She knew my name. How sweet that felt. I stared at her and saw her eyes darting between my hair and my mouth.

"Your name," she said, letting the words drip from her mouth like a cloud of perfume, "is Ginger Cage!" She turned round to face the crowd, squealing with delight as her prepared punch line landed with perfect timing. The playground erupted with laughter.

I tried to look like I was laughing too. But I'd have rather been punched in the face. I felt like I had.

Not what you would call bullying or persecution for the sake of righteousness, though, right?

I'm sure most of you reading this can identify: Our stories can be hard, but they don't really involve persecution. Nothing like the stories of the brave ones in far-off lands facing untold suffering and hardship for following this different way that Jesus teaches us. I'm just little old me, now living in Tennessee, in an area with nine hundred churches. It's way too comfortable. Certainly this announcement isn't for me, is it?

And to a certain extent, it's true. I mean, what these brothers and sisters are facing thousands of miles away really is persecution, and of course God is with *them*. Of course he is on their side, and we must keep them in our minds and prayers as we ache for things to change.

But if we read this and immediately think it's about someone else, then we have missed the point.

PEOPLE OF PERSECUTION

This beatitude, the announcement that *you're blessed when your commitment to God provokes persecution*, is one that I probably wrestle with the most for two reasons.

First, we only have to keep an eye on our news feeds to see that it's not only Christians who are persecuted around the world. There are so many people from all different kinds of religious and ethnic backgrounds, including Christians, who are suffering the worst kinds of persecution because they were born in the wrong place or into the wrong tribe.

So I wrestle with this because I want to tell all their stories. But at the same time, I want to be true to the text: Jesus the Teacher says, "Because of righteousness" and "Because of me." I think the layers of the text include all who are persecuted. But for this book I want to talk about what it looks like to live a life of faith that is worthy of persecution.

Second, I wrestle because what I have come to understand about the Beatitudes is that they are predominantly blessings of God's presence for people in bad situations, and not a list of spiritual virtues to attain—like we've talked about before, they're about being, not doing. But the thing is, I'm also discovering that these are not only passive announcements.

In the Bible, we pay special attention to the moments of the God story that happen on mountains—they are like signposts for us. Some scholars see Jesus in the Sermon on the Mount as a new Moses leading a new Exodus and giving us a new set of commandments.

If we listen, we find the comfort of presence in our poverty, grief, lack of power, and hunger for justice—but we will also hear a prophetic call to action to show mercy, to live with an undivided heart, to be peacemakers. That's why I spend so much time telling the stories of others who are responding to issues of poverty, oppression, injustice, and conflict in the world. Lives full of grace—and also action. Action that comes not from trying to achieve a blessing or status, but action that is compelled because of grace.

In some way our Teacher announces that this gospel is for all the losers, all the broken, all those who haven't normally been included, but who are now included, because God is reordering the way things work and what the world looks like.

For these people—

- the poor in spirit: the people who don't get it, the impoverished, those whose spirits are crushed, those on the B team, the spiritual zeroes, those who keep stumbling
- those who mourn: the brokenhearted, the devastated, the grief-stricken, those familiar with tears
- the meek: the unnoticed, the passed-over, the bullied and marginalized, the discriminated against, those who lack power and choice
- the hungry and thirsty: those haunted by justice, who ache for the shalom of God, for things to be put right, those who feel in their very bones the pain of their own inadequacy to change the way the world works

God meets us in the middle of our poverty, sorrow, struggle, and lack, and announces, "I am on your side."

He meets us there. We don't have to climb a ladder. We don't have to claw our way to the top.

Here at the bottom is where the blessing is.

It's upside-down.

It's confronting.

We don't expect it.

We don't deserve it.

All is grace.

All is mercy.

And if God blesses me at the bottom, in my failure, it changes—if I let it—how I interact with everyone else in the world. If God meets me in my own mess and lack and ache, in my wrestling and in the moments that I keep messing up, then it changes not only me but how I see others who are in the middle of their own messy, broken, and hurting lives.

I can begin to judge less and see myself in others who are struggling, and extend the grace I've received to them.

This lets us *be* in the world in a different way. To begin to show *mercy* to others. To begin spreading it around. So as we live a little more with mercy, our *hearts* become a little more whole and a little more *pure*. And as we offer that to others, we see people how God sees them, and we begin to see God in a new way.

As we see the world differently, we can resist the urge to go take sides, even though that's the path of least resistance. When we find ourselves living as *peacemakers* in the world, this kind of living so easily leads to *persecution* because we all know the way the world works—it wants us to pick a side and it's not going to go down so well when we don't pick a side and we want to see everyone flourish.

And so then we find ourselves not being picked for a side, because fear runs the show, and saying and showing with our lives that love actually casts out fear—well, that's pretty bad for business.

So persecution for us might not look like it does for others in far-off lands. It might just be that we are excluded from the dominant story of the dominant culture. And it can be pretty painful as we are shunned and put to the side.

The way of the Beatitudes doesn't promise us that we'll look good and get invited to be a part of the most popular parties or conferences.

But what I read in Frederick Dale Bruner's commentary on Matthew's Gospel has stuck with me: The promises that tag the first and eighth beatitudes are the same—"theirs is the kingdom of heaven."[4]

It might have been a clever first-century sermon trick to help the listeners remember the Beatitudes, or it could be that Matthew is showing us that we end up in the same place as we started: that through suffering a pushback for our faith, we are brought back to the place of brokenness and the lack and the ache and the poverty of spirit—and the "theirs is the kingdom of heaven."

It starts and ends at the bottom. It can never be about "Look what I've done."

There are all kinds of situations we may find ourselves in. Maybe there will be times when we are trying to be a Jesus presence in the world and we'll find ourselves saying, "Is this even worth it?"

Am I seriously going to try to do the right thing here?

Can I forgive this person?

Is it possible to stay faithful to my wife or husband right now?

Am I going to show mercy and not judgment here?

My friends are going to think I'm stupid.

The world is going to think I'm a prude and a religious nutcase.

Does trying to live the way Jesus teaches screw everything up?

Does it mean that as a disciple I will always be brought back to a place of suffering and powerlessness?

Do I really want to go through with this?

If I follow this Jesus way, will I get what he got?

Well, in some measure—probably.

The story of the Beatitudes is an upside-down story. It promises presence, but it's not always going to be comfortable.

THE ILLUSION OF COMFORT

If you are like me, you actually like your place of comfort and safety, but something's changing and there's an uncomfortable pull to a different life. It's like we breathe different air up the mountain.

But it's a wrestle, because the words of the Sermon on the Mount are constantly chipping away at my soul. At times breaking through and allowing the light of mercy to shine into my deepest places.

The stories of the people who have followed the way of Jesus for most of the last two thousand years have not been either safe or comfortable, and it's not like we should beat ourselves up when our story is not like theirs or we feel like we can never live up to what they did. But we can look to their lives as examples of what it can look like for us to live out these incredible ideas of nonviolence and forgiveness and mercy.

There are dominant powers and stories at work in the world we live in. For us in the West, it's things like advertising, money, consumerism, celebrity, greed, sex, violence, and power. These things fight to get us to collude with them, and because most people in our culture actually do, we find ourselves sticking out like a sore thumb and at odds with them if we dare to try to live a different way.

I was watching an episode of *Sonic Highways,* where Dave Grohl and Foo Fighters were exploring the Washington, DC, music scene that Grohl grew up in. What was inspiring to me wasn't so much the music—the go-go and punk, which was incredible—but the story. How Charles Dickens called Washington, DC, "the City of Magnificent Intentions."[5] How this most affluent city with its magnificent monuments to the idealism of the nation has a gaping wound at its heart. The rebellion and desire for change in the hard-core and punk music scene in the '80s inspired activist and author Mark Andersen, and he started the Positive Force movement after arriving in DC and seeing so many homeless people asking for money. The movement began as a place for a group of misfits, people who didn't feel accepted as part of the dominant society. They found an expression through music and protest, through the sense that if you see something that needs doing, don't wait for anyone else—go and do it.

I finished watching the episode and was left with questions pounding in my head. What am I an activist for? What am I resisting? Who am I speaking out for?

And if I speak out, will there be a pushback? Maybe no one will understand. Maybe I won't fit in.

But maybe another way to read this beatitude is:

Blessed are the misfits,
Blessed are the misunderstood.

SWIMMING UPSTREAM

Someone I actually met in DC for the first time is my friend Jeremy Courtney. Jeremy is an American who has lived in Iraq since 2006, because he felt the urge to help those who were suffering because of war. He moved there with his wife and child and a baby on the way while the U.S.-led coalition forces were still dropping bombs.[6]

Not very comfortable. Not very safe.

A man brought a young girl to Jeremy and said, "Please, please, help my daughter. She's dying." She needed heart surgery. Jeremy didn't know what to do other than investigate the options, but in the end he somehow helped her get surgery. And he then learned that untold thousands of children across Iraq were in similar need, waiting in line for heart surgery in a country without a qualified pediatric heart surgeon.

The effects of posttraumatic stress on pregnant mothers in Iraq and their unborn babies is unbelievable. Thousands of children are being born with a variety of medical conditions because of war—the most common being holes in their hearts.

It's worth pausing here for a moment to think about the fact that the trauma of war affects the very core of life . . . the heart.

With the help of their closest friends, Jeremy and his wife dived into the chaos to save the lives of as many as they could, but sending children abroad proved to be expensive and cumbersome, and it failed to make an impact on the systemic needs of Iraqi hospitals—the places where these children really should be saved.

So despite facing fatwas, death threats, bombings, imprisonments, and intense living conditions, Jeremy and his team have persevered to overcome years of hostilities and distrust in an effort to decrease the backlog of thousands of Iraqi children waiting in line for much-needed heart surgery.

Jeremy's life is about peacemaking and reconciliation and interfaith dialogue and nonviolence and getting aid and health care to those cut off by war and by ISIS (oh yeah—he was there when ISIS came to town). He calls his work Preemptive Love Coalition.

So I know what you're thinking. *Here we go again. This is about another one of those brave heroes who are not like us. Way to make us feel like we don't measure up.*

But trust me. I have a point coming. And it's not that you have to be a superhuman doing dangerous work in Iraq to live out this beatitude.

I asked Jeremy when I talked to him on the phone just now, "Why do you do it? Why do you choose to live like this?" He said,

> Really, at the base of it is this core conviction that the love of God as we understand it and tell the story and believe it as told in the life of Jesus is, to me, one of the most beautiful and profound and hopeful and scary and subversive and transformative ways that I could ever imagine living. Honestly, there are times that are incredibly difficult, and I want to give up, and it's hard to believe, but even on those days, I still want to be a part of it. I still want to live that way, I still want to hang all my hopes on it, and I still want to live out of that belief that there is a love big enough to make all things new. So as I get older and go through various seasons of maturing and questioning, I still just hang really closely to the Jesus way and the Jesus vision and the promises that God is really about more than salvation as I knew it growing up. More than just a private, personal salvation. That God is really in the business of the reconciliation of all things—and so, then, if it's true, and if it's possible, then maybe it even

has to include our enemies. It's got to include the bad guys, and it has to implicate myself, and it reminds me that actually I'm not just the good guy and they're the bad guys. Somehow we all have to be brought back into relationship.

I asked him about persecution and what it looks like to him.

There's a risk with this conversation. It's like walking on a razor's edge. There's a way to talk about persecution that sort of gives us permission to become irreverent and jerks when we don't get our own way. Not winsome or loving or creative or culturally engaged, and if we get pushed back we say, "See, they are persecuting us! Look at them—look at what they've done wrong." When the truth is that we're not loving and we're not reaching out.

On the other hand, I don't think that every instance of persecution is the fault of the one being persecuted. There *is* such a thing as persecution. There *is* such a thing as being kind, relevant, loving, and winsome and compassionate and still getting persecuted! So I don't want to play that down, and I certainly don't want to suggest that the only life that matters is like the most extreme version of facing-down-ISIS types. It's neither realistic nor even helpful to think about that, so I think that we hold all those things in tension, and then create a compelling story that says there is a way to live counterculturally inside a place like the UK or America or even perhaps inside the walls of our institutions. There's still a way to swim upstream, and we need more of that.

And so here's my point: Are we swimming upstream? Wherever we find ourselves, there will be a dominant story. And if we live a different way, a Beatitudes kind of way, we will find ourselves swimming against the flow of popular culture.

When we try to live this out, some difficult things are going to come our way.

When we try to live this out, even when everybody else isn't: In those moments—

God is on our side.

Jeremy is one of my heroes. And it's easy to hear stories like his and just feel like you will never match up to the things he does. But that is just a distraction. Remember, the Beatitudes are blessings, and Jesus doesn't begin the Sermon on the Mount by telling us things we need to do to earn God's favor. He begins with blessings.

It's a reminder that all is grace! That God hears our cry and that he is on our side. That's the blessing.

So when we feel useless and that we should be making a difference in the world like Jeremy, there's a blessing . . . God is with us.

When we are hungry for justice—for ourselves or others—when we don't know what to do, when we keep failing and everything in us shouts that it should be different, we find the blessing of presence. God is on our side.

In Matthew 5:10 Jesus says, "Persecuted because of righteousness," and if we read on, verse 11 says, "Blessed are you when people insult you, persecute you and falsely say all kinds of evil against you because of me."

"Persecuted . . . because of me." Jesus reminds us to look at how he lived in the world.

Then he says something surprising: "Rejoice and be glad, because great is your reward in heaven, for in the same way they persecuted the prophets who were before you" (Matthew 5:12).

Rejoice and be glad. Seriously?

You mean when I am trying to live the right way by loving and serving and speaking out for goodness and wholeness and choosing to swim upstream, and then I get tested to the point of suffering . . . I'm supposed to rejoice and be glad?

That's what it says!

So I did some asking around and found out the words translated "be glad" come from the Greek word *agalliaō*, which literally means to "leap much!"

The first command Jesus gives us in the Sermon on the Mount is that when we face persecution for trying to live his way, we are to "rejoice" and "leap much." That's really quite funny.

Even when we feel like we are being obedient and true to our convictions. Even when we feel like God is silent and not intervening or breaking into our situations. Even when we feel like we've ripped open our chests and let it all out and there is no response.

The promise is presence. God with us.

WHO ARE WE COLLUDING WITH?

I'm so grateful for friends like Brad Nelson. Not only does he know things like Greek and Hebrew, but in this chapter especially he helped me stay on course and stay true to the text. Before I talked with him, I was going down the road of all the people I could think of who suffer injustices in the world—the brave, super Christian heroes. This chapter was going to be full of stories of those people in far-off lands doing extraordinary things. Stories that are helpful and that I love, but that make me feel a bit small and couldn't be told about me. But this is about me. And about you. And even in the midst of the stories, we can never forget that.

We will all have heroes, but it's not ultimately about them. This is about us and our way of being. And this idea of persecution, this idea of swimming upstream, should cause us to ask a key question:

Who am I colluding with?

Are we colluding with the powers of our culture? Consumerism, greed, money, sex, violence, power, advertising, pushing to be first?

Or are we colluding with the upside-down message of this humble, nonviolent King and his counterintuitive Kingdom message? Are we with the poor, the brokenhearted, the meek, those hungry and thirsty for justice and wholeness? Do we show mercy because we have received mercy, and are our hearts becoming pure and undivided so we're able to see God and the world in a different way, advocating for peace and mutual flourishing?

Rabbi Joseph constantly reminds me that Jesus rooted the Sermon on the Mount in the Leviticus 19 purity codes (it's fascinating to read Leviticus 19 and the Sermon on the Mount side by side). Leviticus 19 starts with God saying, "Be holy because I . . . am holy."

To be holy means to be unique, to be different, to be set apart, and in the Beatitudes, Jesus lays out what this uniqueness looks like. Jesus shows us where God is and what he is doing and invites us to this unexpected life of imitating and following him.

Brad calls the people who hear this invitation and accept it "agents of disruption"—holy troublemakers.

Holy troublemakers are people who are compelled to live a life worthy of a pushback—a life worthy of persecution. They're the people who don't just hear the Beatitudes but who actually become the Beatitudes. They collude with this counterintuitive King and his upside-down message.

They swim upstream.

Testing times come.

They don't get picked for the A team.

They are often misfits and misunderstood.

Holy troublemakers understand that where there's persecution, there is suffering. And when we suffer for the cause of righteousness and justice, we connect with the suffering of the greatest misfit of all time.

• • •

We know about people who have gone before us throughout history and heard the invitation to become holy troublemakers. The prophets and apostles, the mystics who kept the thread of Christianity alive through the Dark Ages. The great cloud of witnesses who, according to Hebrews 12, are cheering us on.

Those who chose the way of kindness and love, standing in the gap for the poorest and the least.

People like Mother Teresa, and her lifetime of serving the poor and the dying. How she wrestled with her calling but found a way to keep going and encouraged us to do "small things with great love."[7]

Like Dr. Martin Luther King Jr., the Baptist minister who

inspired and led the African American civil rights movement in the United States with nonviolent activism and the most beautiful and compelling oratory.

Like Clarence Jordan, a farmer and preacher, and his inspiring Koinonia Farm, a mixed-race community formed in the 1940s in southwest Georgia in the midst of Jim Crow segregation. They faced violent attacks with guns and bombs, cross burnings by the Ku Klux Klan, and constant opposition from the towns and churches around them. Clarence was a New Testament scholar who was passionate about the Sermon on the Mount. He was determined that this community would live out the Jesus way of nonviolence and loving your enemies. The pushback and persecution came because this way of life was so confronting to the segregation of the predominantly white businesses and churches in the South.

And there are so many more stories like these—incredible people who made their mark because of their holy troublemaking ways. But I want to talk about the ones closer to home. The people we know personally, or whose stories we hear about, people who are living in the here and now, although they go unnoticed and uncelebrated by the rest of the world. Each one of them is a champion of a different way of living. These people might not be classic examples of the persecuted, but I'm doing this on purpose. They are examples of what it might look like to collude with the message of the Beatitudes, to swim upstream and therefore live lives worthy of persecution—lives worthy of pushback.

We all have these champions in our lives or at least close by, but as it's my book, I get to introduce you (or reintroduce, as the case may be) to some of mine.

• • •

When I was in my twenties, my mum and dad felt the pull into a different way of living. They sold their family home and started serving in several communities across the UK. Always putting others first without any real thought of a comfortable life for themselves. They gave their lives away. They are now in their eighties. My dad is a cancer survivor. Every night while I was on tour and he was having treatment, I lit a candle for him while playing the song "Miracle Maker." I prayed through my guitar. My parents have no real retirement plan to speak of, but they are living a happy life, still loving God and serving people in their community. Never once have I heard them complain or regret any choice they made in terms of giving their lives and security and comfort away, and when it comes to their children and grandchildren, they tell us not only to dream big, but to live our dreams. To go for it. I think they're biased, but they really believe that we can do anything!

Sometimes holy troublemakers don't make the headlines. Sometimes their stories don't make the papers. Sometimes their holy troublemaking just means living a quiet life of radical love.

• • •

Remember Becca Stevens? She's an Episcopal priest and the founder of Thistle Farms, which is the largest social enterprise run by survivors of trafficking, prostitution, abuse, and addiction in the United States. We got introduced to their work earlier. Becca, who is also a survivor of abuse, is the kind of person who embodies something of the hope and mercy of the divine. She sees desperate and broken lives bristling with possibility, and she's a global voice for women's freedom and a champion of the marginalized. The fact that her enterprise is built around thistles shows you something of the way she works: Thistles, which are considered weeds and things to be discarded, have such a beautiful flower, and a deep root, and a strength that can break through concrete. Becca believes that love is the most powerful source for social change in the world. She says that love informs everything she does: "I'm not called to change the world. I am called to love it."[8]

Rev. Becca Stevens is the coolest priest I know!

Sometimes holy troublemakers embrace what the world calls unlovable and collude with the power of love that changes everything.

• • •

We first met Scott Roley way back when we talked about the meek—the guy who as an eleven-year-old heard Dr. King's "I have a dream" speech. I met Scott for the first time after hearing him speak at our church, and I got in touch because I wanted to learn about his work with the poor and with racial equality in our town.

What I didn't know was how meeting Scott would seriously rock my world. Even now, I can't fully tell you the impact his story is having on me.

Scott spent years as a travelling musician, and then as a pastor of Christ Community, a large church in Franklin, Tennessee. Then, along with his friend Michael Card, he saw a video about the work and story of Dr. John Perkins in Mississippi and was stunned and inspired by Dr. Perkins's three Rs of community development. Dr. Perkins says you need to relocate, you need to reconcile, and you need to redistribute. And Scott took him seriously.

In 1997 Scott and his family, having adopted two African American boys, moved into a low-income African American neighborhood in Franklin called Hard Bargain. At first the people thought he was a narcotics cop, because why would a white guy move into this part of town?

Scott jokes, "I told them it was worse—I'm a pastor."[9]

In the years since, Scott has helped rebuild some of the falling-down homes in his neighborhood through his Hard Bargain Association. Giving people a chance of affordable living is vital to stop what Scott calls the "gentrification" of the poor areas of Franklin, which sits in Williamson County, the wealthiest county in Tennessee.

Along with friends from both white and African American communities, Scott has spearheaded an extraordinary work, one based on the actual needs of the community rather than what we might think the needs are. Scott, along with an amazing woman named Paige Overton Pitts, started a pediatric health clinic and also New Hope Academy, a school serving preschool to sixth grade, giving low-income kids a chance of empowerment and choice when it comes to education.

Scott has spent so much time driving me around Franklin, showing me neighborhoods, telling me stories, introducing me to new friends. I remember him tearing up as we were talking one day—he couldn't believe someone was interested in his work. Scott is humble but determined, focused and single-minded when it comes to serving the poor and the marginalized.

Scott says, "Loving your neighbor is not hard—it just costs you your life!"[10]

Sometimes holy troublemakers see their privilege and set it aside so they can give their lives for racial equality and the poor.

• • •

I want to tell you about my friend Daniel White. A humanitarian photographer and artist liaison for Food for the Hungry, based in Nashville, he connects recording artists with the work of sponsoring children in areas around the world that are often too far off the beaten track for most NGOs. This work has captured Daniel's heart and soul. Now, as someone who is young, handsome, and a talented photographer and entrepreneur, Daniel could be off somewhere else making his fortune. He was named in *Nashville Business Journal* as one of the featured "40 under 40"[11] and has incredible offers from the commercial and advertising world. But his work with Food for the Hungry and these kids has changed his life. He knows what it's like to chase fame and fortune but doesn't like the person he becomes when pursuing these things. He says that his life just feels off when it becomes all about him. But when life includes serving the poorest of the poor, he just feels a bit more whole as a human. That's his barometer. He says that of course making money isn't in itself bad—but when it's the only focus, it knocks him off track.

What I love about the work of Food for the Hungry is that, yes, it is about getting as many children as possible sponsored—but in every community Food for the Hungry works in, all the people benefit. The kids get a chance in life, but the whole community is helped with clean water, schools, clinics, and ways to create businesses and become self-sustaining.

Karen and I travelled with Daniel and Food for the Hungry

on a trip we will never forget and saw with our own eyes once again the poorest of the poor who welcome you with a joy that you never can understand. You really do see God in their eyes. We are committed to help Food for the Hungry any way we can in their vital work of serving the poor.[12]

• • •

Then there's my friend Shane.

Shane Claiborne is a guy who, true to Matthew 5:12, rejoices and leaps so much, it's infectious. Based in North Philly, Shane is someone who also takes seriously Dr. Perkins's encouragement to relocate reconcile, and redistribute, Shane is a part of a community called the Simple Way. I'll let him tell you about it.

> Basically I got up here to go to school, and while we were in school we kind of had an interruption. We had a group of these homeless moms and kids that were living in a church, an abandoned church that's a couple miles from here, and getting involved in that is what kind of sparked the movement that gave birth to the Simple Way. We were really inspired by the early church. The book of Acts, Acts 2 and 4, everybody's sharing what they had, no one's claiming any of their possessions. Of course Mother Teresa was a part of that—her whole "doing small things with great love."
>
> So a lot of our work started with really simple, warm hospitality. Folks that were homeless coming and having a meal together here, and kids coming to get help with homework. We still do a lot of that stuff, but I think what it evolved into over the last eighteen years is the whole compassion-leads-to-justice kind of thing, where we ended

up saying, "Well, let's also try to do something about why so many folks are homeless and why masses of people are living in poverty when a handful of people live however they want." It's about things like mass incarceration and gun violence, the stuff that's destroying people's lives. That's very deeply connected to our faith, you know.

I grew up Deep South, God and country, but then living in North Philly, where violence is one of the monsters that we really wrestle with, I began to get inspired by a lot of Dr. King. I told the kids in the ghettos that violence won't solve their problems, but then they ask me, "Why does the government use it?" And I couldn't speak against the violence to the kids in the ghettos without speaking against the violence of my government, so that's really what I try to do. A consistency of life is a framework for what we do. It's a really helpful umbrella, and I think that's something that's resonating with a lot of people. It's been a regular part of the Catholics and the Mennonites and others, but also I think a lot of evangelicals. I think a consistent ethic of life is real helpful language and framework because it says, "Yeah, we do care that black lives matter, we do care about abortion, we do care about the death penalty. These are all things that are destroying people's lives, and God cares about that. God is the author of life."

We love creativity. We love prophetic imagination. We like to interrupt the stuff that's destroying people. We love hanging out with kids and planting gardens and making broken and forgotten places beautiful.

We started as six college friends. We bought a house together, so we were piled in a three-room row house kind of deal—and what we grew into is more of a village now. The way I've started to come to look at it is we started an intentional community in the neighborhood, but we've become community with the neighborhood. So a lot of the people on the block that have been here longer than me would say they are the Simple Way, and they're leading a lot of the stuff that we do. It's more of a village than an intentional community now and there's a whole lot of appendages to it.[13]

Then Shane and I talked about the Beatitudes:

The Beatitudes transcend the very stale and tiring debate of faith and works. It's who we are and it's who Christ is— and yet when you look at these announcements, they're in contrast to the values that we've come to adore and admire, like power and money and empire building, which are everywhere. If you came up with a set of statements that were the antithesis of the dominant powers of America and our cultural values, it would sound like love—it's meekness, it's the poor, it's the merciful. When you look at the Beatitudes especially, and just allow them to speak for themselves, in contrast to the political debates and everything else, it's really interesting.

In the Beatitudes, there's a certain way of emphasizing what's been neglected. When I look at Scripture and the image of the mighty being cast from their thrones, the lowly lifted up, the mountains being laid low and the valleys lifted up, there's this sort of dual trajectory in the Kingdom. Desmond Tutu says, "Setting the oppressed free from being oppressed and the oppressors free from oppressing."

I'm sure some people would say, "Well, blessed are the poor—but doesn't God wanna bless the rich, too? Or blessed are the meek, but doesn't God love the proud?" What I like to say is it's like when saying black lives matter. It doesn't mean other lives don't matter, and saying black is beautiful doesn't mean white people are ugly. But it's emphasizing something. I think that's what the Beatitudes do too. They are stressing what all other evidence would point towards, and they stand in contradiction. So when the dominant culture says that meek people actually don't matter, Jesus is saying, "No, meek people are blessed. They're at the heart of God."

Because Shane is an activist, at times his work rubs up against the law of the land. I asked him some of the ways his allegiance to the way of the Beatitudes has been tested.

Yeah, we're not short of those stories! One time, one of my eighty-year-old friends, Sister Margaret—she's a nun—and I had gone to jail so many times that we got sentenced to go to citizenship training to be better law-abiding citizens!

At the time, there were executions in Pennsylvania, so we had chained ourselves to the governor's mansion to try to prevent the death penalty from moving forward. But then we also were largely getting arrested every week at the time for the anti-homeless laws that made it illegal to sleep in the parks and illegal to feed people. We had open sleep-outs and demonstrations against those laws. We probably got arrested ten to fifteen times during those, but we won in court.

It was Saint Augustine who said, "An unjust law is no law at all." It's proven itself true over and over. People will always point to Romans 13 as saying we're meant to submit to authority, right? I've come to know that there are two ways of submitting to authority. One is obeying the good laws, and the other one is openly suffering the consequences of disobeying the bad laws respectfully. I don't think to submit means obey all the time. I think this is one of the ways that we've seen the world change when it comes to civil rights and the Underground Railroad and all these things. What one of our judges even said when we went to trial was that we weren't criminals—we were freedom fighters.

What civil disobedience does and can do is, like Dr. King said, "expose injustice so that it becomes so uncomfortable that people can't help but respond." What happens when we respectfully suffer for breaking the unjust laws and exposing injustice is that it brings that to the surface. When you see black folks being squirted with water hoses and dogs put on them, it raises the question—What is evil here?

At the time before the regime in Iraq was overthrown, Shane and a group of doctors travelled to Iraq to help relieve the incredible difficulty imposed upon everyday citizens of that country. Sanctions had weakened the infrastructure of the nation so that the military could be defeated, but it had a devastating effect on the civilian population.

When we came back from Iraq, technically some of the things that we did were illegal because it broke U.S. sanctions. It was illegal for us to take medication to Iraq, but we did it openly, and when we got back some of the doctors actually went to trial. They faced twelve years in prison for taking medication to Iraq. It was so mind boggling that the average person saw that and was like, this is insane!

Even the judge said the state has a very difficult case to prove if we are going to argue that doctors who are going to volunteer in Iraqi hospitals and take medication should go to jail, and so what it did was it exposed that. Ultimately no one ended up going to jail, but people did begin to pay attention to the injustice of the sanctions and the war.

It was fantastic though, because the group was fined $20,000—and they paid it in Iraqi dinar. So what would have been $20,000 totally just deteriorated and devalued to the point that this pile of cash was worth $8. I love it because it's what John Yoder calls revolutionary subordination. That's exactly the work we've gotta do with things like the weapon conversations here in the States. That prophetic imagination that says we're not gonna change people's minds by arguing with them, we're gonna change people's minds by winning over their hearts and by amplifying the pain.

So when you see a mom, who lost her kid to a gun, transforming that gun into a tool to use in a garden, there's something visceral and powerful and mystical that happens. It's hard to argue with that, so that's our goal. To try to use the imagination to amplify the pain to expose the injustice and also to point towards a better world.

Shane vehemently opposes the death penalty and is campaigning for its absolute abolishment. He frames everything around this conversation with grace and redemption. That no one is beyond mercy, that mercy triumphs over judgment. He says,

The pope has called for world abolition of the death penalty and, well, I believe it's gonna happen. I would just love for evangelicals to not miss the boat and instead be on the forefront of it. There's a lot of really great signs that you're probably well aware of. The Pew study, I think it was, that showed 80 percent of millennial Christians are against the penalty—and it's not in spite of their faith, it's actually *because* of it. They read stuff like the Beatitudes, and they're going, "Blessed are the merciful . . . hm—that seems hard to legitimize the death penalty!" Every pro-life Christian should consider what life means with the death penalty.[14]

Sometimes holy troublemakers take the message of the Beatitudes so seriously they get arrested for it.

• • •

So once again: When you read these stories, please don't go making it about "them" or counting yourself out of the picture because "there's no way I can do that." It's not about the "super Christians"—this is about me and it's about you, right where we are at, right here and right now.

So what does it actually look like for the rest of us?

I think we have to start by asking ourselves some hard questions:

- Who and what am I colluding with? The dominant powers at play in the world—or the one who shared the message of the Beatitudes?

- What am I resisting?

- Are there situations in everyday life where I'm being forced to go with the flow? What would happen if I said no?

- Who am I speaking out for? The homeless in my town? The woman at work on the receiving end of sexual jibes? The effeminate guy at school who's getting bullied?

- If I speak out—if I resist—am I willing to suffer for it? Because it might just happen.

And the words from the hill are speaking still: "You are blessed, God is on your side."

This isn't about striving to get persecuted. The Beatitudes are about receiving the grace that in our own poverty, brokenness, lack of power, and ache for justice we can hear the amazing, exuberant, counterintuitive announcement that God is on our side.

Maybe we need to do the absolutely necessary internal work

- of showing ourselves mercy
- of lifting our own heads
- of not beating ourselves up
- of healing our divided hearts
- of receiving the gift of peace on the inside

And when we do, I believe the prophetic call to action to love God with all our heart and soul and mind, and to love our neighbor as ourselves, will follow.

I never met Mother Teresa, but I know people who knew her. They tell me she was a giant of a human inside a tiny frame, serious about love, mercy, and justice winning in the here and now. They say that the way she loved, the way she valued human life, the way she fought for dignity for the dying, was confronting and disrupting. They say her sense of humor was sharp and cheeky.

So it seems fitting to end this chapter, which is essentially about swimming upstream, with some words this holy troublemaker pinned to the wall of the Shishu Bhavan, her children's home in Kolkata.

People are unreasonable, illogical, and self-centered,
LOVE THEM ANYWAY

• • •

If you do good, people will accuse you
of selfish, ulterior motives,
DO GOOD ANYWAY

• • •

If you are successful, you win false friends and true enemies,
SUCCEED ANYWAY

• • •

The good you do will be forgotten tomorrow,
DO GOOD ANYWAY

• • •

Honesty and frankness make you vulnerable,
BE HONEST AND FRANK ANYWAY

• • •

What you spend years building may be
destroyed overnight,
BUILD ANYWAY

• • •

People really need help but
may attack you if you help them,
HELP PEOPLE ANYWAY

• • •

Give the world the best you have and
you'll get kicked in the teeth,
**GIVE THE WORLD THE BEST
YOU'VE GOT ANYWAY**[15]

"Blessed are those who are persecuted because of righteousness, for theirs is the kingdom of heaven."

THE VIEW
FROM UP HERE

I'VE COME BACK to the Holy Land, and I'm sitting once again on the hillside overlooking Galilee, where tradition and scholars say that Jesus spoke these words. It's my third time here. I love it. Each time, there's a sense of coming home.

To my right I can see the city of Tiberias, which was founded by Herod Antipas, the son of Herod the Great, and named after the Roman emperor Tiberius in the AD 20. Beyond that into the distance is the land known as the West Bank, the Occupied Territories, or simply Palestine. Ahead of me is the Sea of Galilee, and on the horizon, the mouth of the Jordan River. To my left I can see the hills of the Golan Heights, and beyond there is Syria with all its suffering and chaos right now. If I walk a mile or two down the hillside, I will reach Capernaum, where Peter lived, the scene of so many stories from the Christian Scriptures.

I sit here in the Mediterranean sunshine, thinking and meditating and contemplating life with all its interweaving of people and stories and joy and pain. I've once again been with friends, Israelis and Palestinians, and had a glimpse into their lives, so much that is beautiful and so much that is painful and full of sorrow.

In this extraordinary upside-down teaching of what the Kingdom of God looks like, Jesus gives us a lens with which to look at the world, and I think to myself that here on this hillside is not just the place where our Teacher walked two thousand years ago—it's one of the places where he would walk and talk if he were here today.

And in many ways he is here, wherever people are listening to these words, engaging with one another, and accepting the invitation to be where God is. In the middle of conflict, poverty, brokenness, and people who are hurting, he is here—healing our bodies and our minds; bringing us the message that God is with us; announcing that he has begun the work of redeeming, remaking, and restoring the world, and that we are invited to join in this work. This work will cost us everything, but we keep going because God is on our side.

Remember how we talked about the invitation to listen, to put down our certainty and to pick up curiosity and, in conversation with each other, to go on this journey together?

I hope you can hear this invitation to the unexpected: that you are a vital piece of the puzzle of this divine universe.

In the middle of all the noise and chaos, we can hear this invitation right now. Where we are, with as little or as much as we have in our hands. We don't have to qualify. There's not a set of rules to follow, nothing we have to achieve. Whatever our lives have to offer is vitally important, and we can discover and embrace the reason for our existence and play our part in doing some good in the world as we work this out with each other.

Rabbi Joseph said,

We were the ones who took the invitation to hear the
master teach. He's not on the hill anymore, but the words
we've heard now engage us in conversation. Stu and I
have conversations all the time. Conversations over Skype
and FaceTime and phone. Conversations face-to-face.
Conversations that need little stimulus. I think that's what
the master wanted.

They are conversations and questions that require
us to keep listening. *You think the meek are this, and I
think the persecuted are this—and here's my story about
personally mourning.* What will our conversations help
guide us in doing, if we take the invitation seriously? The
invitation of this project is to engage in the conversations
of difference. I'm going to have to think differently, and
having thought differently, I will engage differently.

Once I've engaged differently, my behavior is going
to be different. We are the ones who have to take up that
prophetic challenge. I'm a Jew. I accepted the invitation,
and I'm thrilled to be on the hill with Christians and
Muslims and maybe some atheists. But we are on the hill.
We've all accepted the invitation to hear the words. To
listen.

I want to think or behave differently; I want to hope
that I will behave with greater mercy, greater depth of
perspective. To remember the widow, the fatherless, the
orphan, and the stranger. Those are not new categories.
Those are categories that Jesus the Judean understood,
when he offered those words on the hill.

Now I get to talk about them with everyone else
who's on the hill. Who knows? Maybe this time we will

listen differently. But those words still challenge us. It's accepting the invitation to the challenge that ultimately will help us all.[1]

Two thousand years ago, Jesus the Jewish rabbi gave this sermon to the people who needed to hear it, and all these years later, I still need to hear it.

• • •

If life is like a jigsaw puzzle, I know for sure I don't have all the pieces. That's why other people and their stories are so important. They are what is known in the Hebrew language as *malach*, which means "messenger" or "one who is sent." We translate this as "angel." Rabbi Lawrence Kushner says that these people rarely know that they are sent or that they even have a message for us.[2] Unsuspecting and unaware, they go about their life doing their work, consumed with their plans and itineraries, unknowing of the fact that they are carrying a divine piece of your puzzle. How many times does it happen that we meet someone, maybe even unexpectedly, and we leave that place and think, *Wow, I needed that!*

I feel this way about everyone I've introduced you to in this book. Each one has given me a unique and perfectly shaped jigsaw piece that fits the puzzle of my life somehow and helps me get that little bit closer to being complete and whole. They have helped me hear and feel and figure out what it could look like for the Beatitudes to be a compass for my life.

As I sit here with you all on the hill pondering, I'm aware that we don't have the man himself, Jesus, here in the flesh. We can't hear for ourselves with our own ears the words coming out of his mouth. We can't stop him and say, "What do you mean the meek inherit the earth? That's ridiculous!"

What we have is the sacred text, this inaugural "state of the universe" address from Jesus. We also have our lives, our conversations, our questions, our experiences, the people and jigsaw pieces from the messengers around us. But it's all so full of surplus meaning and open for interpretation—I mean, what does it actually mean for us? What does it mean for me?

What we want is answers. What we want is certainty.

Jesus doesn't give us that.

What he offers us instead and constantly throughout the Beatitudes is presence, and—if we hear the invitation—an opportunity to *be* present.

"But Jesus, I'm too broken!" *You're blessed. God is with you.*

"But I keep really messing up!" *You're blessed. God is on your side.*

"But I have no clue what to do!" *You're blessed. God is with you.*

"But no one is listening!" *You're blessed. God is on your side.*

We are not invited to a life of certainty. We are invited to a life of curiousness with God beside us.

This is our adventure, to explore and find out what this could mean for us, what life could be like as we are compassionate toward ourselves, and as we extend our circle of compassion and mercy to those around us.

Maybe for you the initial work is internal. Maybe the Beatitudes are a doorway to shift your focus from what is on the outside to what is on the inside. From what is influencing you externally to what is influencing you internally. Maybe the Beatitudes help us see the difference between trying to change ourselves from the outside in and being changed by God from the inside out.

The Beatitudes give us a good framework for that kind of spiritual pursuit, where we empty ourselves of the desire for possessions, the need for pleasure, the obsession with power—and where we allow God to fill us and satisfy us with the things that really matter.

A number of theologians have said that the Beatitudes are the pinnacle and summary of all of Jesus' teaching and what it means to follow him as a disciple. They provide a way or a path to follow that anyone can live at any time, in any circumstance, and in any culture.

For the early followers of Jesus, this was their anthem, their path, and their hope.

I had a really interesting conversation with my friend Tim Day, an author and speaker from Toronto. We talked about the creeds that over the centuries have been written and used in liturgies and prayers. The creeds were written in times of crisis to remind us of what is true and also as a way to halt false doctrine from entering the church.

Tim was saying that the problem with historic creeds we have written for ourselves, like the Apostles' Creed or the Nicene Creed, is that although they are statements of truth and belief, their statements have little impact on how we live or the way we treat other people. It is like saying, "I believe that there is a sun in the sky and earth below. I believe in gravity. I believe the sun makes plants grow. I believe one day I will die." All of these are true. Yet they easily slip into the background of our thinking and rarely shape how we live.

The creeds we wrote for ourselves leave out all of Jesus' teachings and jump from his birth right to his death. And so those of us in the Christian community and tradition can have (as we do) a history of division, oppression, and violence while all the time claiming to be completely orthodox according to our creeds.

Historically, our lives have looked very little like the life described by the Beatitudes. Rather, we have woven our creeds into our liturgies, songs, and sermons, reminding ourselves of their truth on a Sunday morning—and then we have gone back on Monday to fighting a war, beating a slave, executing a criminal, climbing a corporate ladder, hoarding more wealth, building an empire, or looking hatefully at our neighbor or enemy.

What if, like the earliest Jesus followers, we began to see the Beatitudes as the Jesus Creed?

What if the Beatitudes became, once again, our anthem of hope and life?

What if the Beatitudes became the light that shines on the path to a new way of living?

Imagine if we began to sing again the anthem he gave us.

Imagine if this song united us and guided our lives.

Imagine what kind of future we could create.

I think what we need—to use church language—is a revival. But not one that's measured in responses to the message or the number of attendees or souls saved or how loud we shout or how good the music is or how many "miracles" we see.

I believe in miracles, but so many times we cry out for divine intervention when the Beatitudes show us that the Divine is all around us and fully available to us. Sometimes we need to *be* the miracle our neighbour needs. If the blessing in the Beatitudes is God's presence, then the Beatitudes urge us to *be present* to ourselves and to others in a way that imitates God.

In our Delirious? song "Revival Town," Martin wrote,

Well I've got a story to tell
About the King above all kings
You spoke for peace, hope, love and justice
Things that we all need today
You let a broken generation
Become a dancing generation
This is revival generation
You may not hear it on the radio
But you can feel it in the air[3]

That's the kind of revival I long for, when I listen to the words on the hill. A subversive, under-the-radar movement of holy troublemakers living for mercy, peace, hope, love, and justice.

So may we hear these words from the hill—speaking still.

May we remember how to listen.

May we be people who, because we've been offered presence in our brokenness, mercy and forgiveness in our failure—peace, hope, love, and justice—offer these things back to the world.

May we accept this invitation to carry on one step at a time in the middle of whatever life throws at us: our struggles and suffering, our failures, our heartbreaks, our oppression, our desire for justice, our successes and all that we are good at. May we be bringers of mercy with undivided hearts, peacemakers who discover a surprising, rebellious joy when we get pushed back.

And when we feel alone—and when we are misunderstood—and when we don't fit in and when we feel like running away—let's remember that we are a part of something that's numbered in grains of sand and stars in the sky.

You are not alone.

God is on your side.

ENGAGE

I HOPE THAT YOU'VE enjoyed reading this book and that in some small way you feel encouraged and inspired.

Sometimes we read, see, or hear about all this stuff and would really love to get involved—you know, *do* something. We're inspired, but we don't know where to start. First of all, I would say take some deep breaths and let this message really sink in: God is on your side when you haven't got it all together.

Once you've given that some time, if you still feel a pull to some of the great people and organizations I've talked about in this book, and would like to explore the possibility of engaging further, I have just the place for you. Please check out TheBeatitudesProject.com/engage for a comprehensive list with links.

Thank you.

Stu

NOTES

CHAPTER 1: POOR IN SPIRIT

1. "Human Development Report, 2014: Sustaining Human Progress: Reducing Vulnerabilities and Building Resilience," United Nations Development Programme, 2014, http://hdr.undp.org/sites/default/files/hdr14-report-en-1.pdf (accessed August 23, 2016).

2. Deborah Hardoon, Sophia Ayele, and Ricardo Fuentes-Nieva, "An Economy for the 1%," Oxfam, January 18, 2016, https://www.oxfam.org/sites/www.oxfam.org /files/file_attachments/bp210-economy-one-percent-tax-havens-180116-en_0.pdf (accessed August 23, 2016).

3. Elissa Kim, conversation with the author, Bongo Java East, Nashville, TN, January 11, 2016. Used with permission.

4. Ibid.

5. Sam Polk, "For the Love of Money," *New York Times*, January 18, 2014, http:// www.nytimes.com/2014/01/19/opinion/sunday/for-the-love-of-money.html?_r=0 (accessed August 23, 2016).

6. Ibid.

7. Ibid.

8. Ibid.

9. Ibid.

10. Sam Polk, Skype conversation with the author, March 2, 2016. Used with permission.

CHAPTER 2: MOURN

1. David Kessler, interview by Rob Bell, *Robcast 45: Grief, Loss and Joy with David Kessler*, podcast audio, October 18, 2015, http://robbell.podbean.com/e/episode -45-grief-loss-and-joy-with-david-kessler/ (accessed August 23, 2016).

2. Ibid.

3. Al Andrews, conversation with the author, Franklin, TN, February 1, 2016. Used with permission.

4. Brad Nelson, conversation with the author, 2015. Used with permission.

5. Kessler, *Robcast 45: Grief, Loss and Joy with David Kessler.*

6. Martin Sheen, interview by Krista Tippett, "Spirituality of Imagination," *On Being with Krista Tippett*, podcast audio, December 16, 2015, http://www.onbeing.org /program/martin-sheen-spirituality-of-imagination/8257 (accessed August 23, 2016).

CHAPTER 3: MEEK

1. Simon and Garfunkel, "Blessed," *Sounds of Silence* © 1966, Columbia.

2. Scott Roley, conversation with the author, Franklin, TN, March 22, 2016. Used with permission.

3. Tangie Lane, conversation with the author, Franklin, TN, March 22, 2016. Used with permission.

4. "The 'Last Lynching': How Far Have We Come?" NPR, October 13, 2008, http://www.npr.org/templates/story/story.php?storyId=95672737 (accessed August 23, 2016).

5. Charles Robinson, conversation with the author, Franklin, TN, March 22, 2016. Used with permission.

6. "Tribal Nations and the United States: An Introduction," National Congress of American Indians, http://www.ncai.org/about-tribes (accessed October 3, 2016).

7. "Preserving Native American Languages," The Leadership Conference, http:// www.civilrights.org/indigenous/language/ (accessed October 3, 2016).

8. Guenter Lewy, "Were American Indians the Victims of Genocide?" History News Network, September 2004, http://historynewsnetwork.org/article/7302 (accessed August 23, 2016).

9. "Global Trends: Forced Displacement in 2015," the UN Refugee Agency, 2016, http://www.unhcr.org/576408cd7.pdf (accessed August 23, 2016).

10. Laurence Topham, "Family Life in a Syrian Refugee Camp," *The Guardian*, July 25, 2013, https://www.theguardian.com/world/video/2013/jul/25/family -life-syrian-refugee-camp-video (accessed August 23, 2016).

11. Fady Al-Hagal, conversation with the author, February 2016. Used with permission.

12. Alex Altman, "A Syrian Refugee Story," *Time*, November 20, 2015, http://time .com/a-syrian-refugee-story/ (accessed August 23, 2016).

13. Ibid.

14. Ibid.

15. Ibid.

16. Riyad Al-Kasem, conversation with the author, Café Rakka, Hendersonville, TN, March 15, 2016. Used with permission.

17. James Grady, conversation with the author, Brentwood, TN, March 21, 2016. Used with permission.
18. I like how Gabe Lyons and David Kinnaman in their book *Good Faith* talk about something they call "confident pluralism." We live in a pluralistic and diverse society, and Gabe and David really lay out a way to engage this cultural moment for the common good while still being people of good faith. I recommend you read their book if this is something you are wrestling with.

CHAPTER 4: HUNGER AND THIRST
1. Frederick Dale Bruner, *Matthew: A Commentary*, vol. 1, The Christbook, Matthew 1–12 (Grand Rapids, MI: Eerdmans, 2004), 155.
2. N. T. Wright, *Matthew for Everyone: Part 1, Chapters 1–15*, (Louisville, KY: Westminster John Knox Press, 2004), 36.
3. Thomas Merton, *Thoughts in Solitude* (New York: Farrar, Straus and Giroux, 1958), 79.
4. Pope Francis, *The Name of God Is Mercy*, trans. Oonagh Stransky (New York: Random House, 2016), 25–26.
5. Radiohead, "Everything in Its Right Place," *Kid A* © Capitol, 2000.
6. "Global Trends: Forced Displacement in 2015," the UN Refugee Agency, 2016, http://www.unhcr.org/576408cd7.pdf (accessed August 23, 2016).
7. Jared Noetzel, conversation with the author, Washington DC, July 16, 2016. Used with permission.
8. "Highest Income Counties in 2011," *Washington Post*, September 20, 2012, http://www.washingtonpost.com/wp-srv/special/local/highest-income-counties/ (accessed August 23, 2016).
9. Galatians 6:2, ESV.
10. Darren Whitehead, conversation with the author, Franklin, TN, June 16, 2016. Used with permission.
11. Dr. John Perkins, quoted by Daniel Hill, "My favorite CCDA quotes – Dr. John Perkins," *Daniel Hill's Blog*, September 29, 2014, https://pastordanielhill.com /2014/09/29/my-favorite-ccda-quotes-dr-john-perkins/.

CHAPTER 5: MERCY
1. Bruner, *Matthew: A Commentary*, 165.
2. Bruner, Matthew, 155.
3. Pope Francis, *The Name of God Is Mercy*, 85.
4. *Oxford Dictionaries*, s.v. "mercy," accessed October 16, 2016, https://en.oxford dictionaries.com/definition/mercy.
5. Rabbi Joseph Edelheit, Skype conversation with the author, March 28, 2016. Used with permission.
6. Rev. Becca Stevens, conversation with the author, Nashville, TN, September 22, 2016. Used with permission.
7. Regina Mullins, conversation with the author, Nashville, TN, March 24, 2016. Used with permission.

8. Jennifer Clinger, conversation with the author, Nashville, TN, September 16, 2016. Used with permission.

9. There is an amazing movement in the trucking world to fight against trafficking. To find out more, please check out http://www.truckersagainsttrafficking.org/.

10. "Ricky Jackson freed from prison after 39 years for wrongful murder conviction," YouTube video, 4:49, posted by "cleveland.com," November 21, 2014, https://www.youtube.com/watch?v=2yV_HLDjMlw.

11. Gaile Owens, conversation with the author, Nashville, TN, August 25, 2015. Used with permission.

12. You can read the full story of what happened in Stephen Owens's book *Set Free* (Nashville: B&H, 2013)

13. Amy Grant, conversation with the author, Nashville, TN, August 25, 2015. Used with permission.

14. This quote has changed and evolved into many versions over the years. The original quote is from Ian MacLaren: "Be pitiful, for every man is fighting a hard battle." "Be Kind; Everyone You Meet Is Fighting a Hard Battle," Quote Investigator, http://quoteinvestigator.com/2010/06/29/be-kind/ (accessed October 5, 2016).

CHAPTER 6: PURE IN HEART

1. Thanks to Tim Day, who helped me see this story like this.

2. Chris Rea, "Just Passing Through," *On the Beach* © Geffen, 1986.

3. C. S. Lewis, *Mere Christianity* (New York: HarperCollins, 2015), 103, 122–123.

4. Richard Rohr and John Bookser Feister, *Jesus' Plan for a New World* (Cincinnati, OH: St. Anthony Messenger Press, 1996), 87.

5. José González, "Stay Alive," *The Secret Life of Walter Mitty* © Peermusic Publishing, Sony/ATV Music Publishing LLC, Warner/Chappell Music, Inc., 2013.

6. Abraham Joshua Heschel, *The Sabbath* (New York: Farrar, Straus and Giroux, 1951), 9.

7. "Desmond Tutu's message to activists: Good will prevail," YouTube video, 1:35, posted by "The Elders," August 26, 2009, https://www.youtube.com/watch?v=FIIqAMFWIwE.

CHAPTER 7: PEACEMAKERS

1. Walter Wink, "The Myth of Redemptive Violence," *The Bible in Transmission*, Spring 1999, http://www2.goshen.edu/~joannab/women/wink99.pdf (accessed August 23, 2016).

2. Todd Deatherage, conversation with the author, Jerusalem, Israel, February 2016. Used with permission.

3. Robi Damelin, conversations with the author, Jerusalem, Israel, June 2013 and February 2016. Used with permission.

4. "About Us," Holy Land Trust, http://www.holylandtrust.org/about-holy-land-trust.html (accessed September 27, 2016).

5. Sami Awad, conversation with the author, Bethlehem, Palestine, February 2016. Used with permission.

CHAPTER 8: PERSECUTED

1. Janelle P., "Young Syrian Christians Explain Why They Didn't Flee the War," Open Doors, March 10, 2016, https://www.opendoorsusa.org/christian-persecution /stories/tag-blog-post/young-syrian-christians-explain-why-they-didnt-flee-the -war/ (accessed August 23, 2016).
2. Janelle P., "Burkina Faso Dead Include 7 Mission Workers," Open Doors, January 24, 2016, https://www.opendoorsusa.org/take-action/pray/tag-prayer-updates-post /burkina-faso-dead-include-7-mission-workers/ (accessed August 23, 2016).
3. Harriet Sherwood, "Christians flee growing persecution in Africa and Middle East," *The Guardian*, January 12, 2016, http://www.theguardian.com/ world/2016/jan/13/christians-flee-growing-persecution-africa-middle-east (accessed August 23, 2016).
4. Bruner, *Matthew*, 181.
5. Charles Dickens, *American Notes for General Circulation* (London: Penguin, 2000), 129.
6. Jeremy Courtney, phone conversation with the author, March 28, 2016. Used with permission.
7. "Mother Teresa: Do small things with great love," Catholic News Service, September 4, 2016, http://www.catholicnews.com/services/englishnews/2016 /mother-teresa-do-small-things-with-great-love.cfm.
8. "Advocate, author Becca Stevens to speak on 'Living Out Love,'" Emory News Center, October 14, 2013, http://news.emory.edu/stories/2013/10/upress_becca _stevens_candler_forum/campus.html (accessed October 3, 2016).
9. Scott Roley, conversation with the author, Franklin, TN, March 22, 2016. Used with permission.
10. Ibid.
11. "NBJ announces our 2016 40 Under 40 winners," *Nashville Business Journal*, January 26, 2016, http://www.bizjournals.com/nashville/blog/2016/01/nbj -announces-our2016-40-under-40-winners.html#g38.
12. Daniel is an incredible photographer, and he documents his life and work through his camera's eye. You can follow along on Instagram @danielcwhite.
13. Shane Claiborne, Skype conversation with the author, February 23, 2016. Used with permission.
14. Shane wrote a book about the death penalty called *Executing Grace* (San Francisco: HarperOne, 2016). Visit the website at http://executinggrace.com/.
15. Mother Teresa, *A Simple Path* (New York: Ballantine, 1995), 185.

OUTRO: THE VIEW FROM UP HERE

1. Rabbi Joseph Edelheit, conversation with the author, Minneapolis, MN, June 8, 2016. Used with permission.
2. Rabbi Lawrence Kushner, *Honey from the Rock* (Woodstock, VT: Jewish Lights, 2000), 68.
3. Delirious?, "Revival Town," *King of Fools* © Furious? Records, 1997.

A BOOK, ALBUM, AND FILM, ALL INSPIRED
BY THE ANNOUNCEMENTS KNOWN AS THE BEATITUDES.
FEATURING THE WRITING AND PERFORMING TALENTS OF:

AMY GRANT, MICHAEL W. SMITH, JOHN MARK McMILLAN,
MATT MAHER, AMANDA COOK, AUDREY ASSAD,
ALL SONS & DAUGHTERS, MARTIN SMITH, THE BRILLIANCE,
TERRIAN BASS, ANTHONY SKINNER, PROPAGANDA, AND STU G.

THEBEATITUDESPROJECT.COM

CP1214